JEFFERSON DAVIS AND THE CIVIL WAR ERA

JEFFERSON DAVIS AND THE CIVIL WAR ERA

WILLIAM J. COOPER, JR.

>|<

Louisiana State University Press
Baton Rouge

PUBLISHED WITH THE ASSISTANCE OF THE V. RAY CARDOZIER FUND

Published by Louisiana State University Press
Copyright © 2008 by Louisiana State University Press
Manufactured in the United States of America
First printing

DESIGNER: Michelle A. Neustrom
TYPEFACE: Adobe Caslon Pro
PRINTER AND BINDER: Thomson-Shore, Inc.

LIBRARY OF CONGRESS CATALOGING-IN-PUBLICATION DATA

Cooper, William J. (William James), 1940–
    Jefferson Davis and the Civil War era / William J. Cooper, Jr.
        p. cm.
    Includes index.
    ISBN 978-0-8071-3371-2 (cloth : alk. paper) 1. Davis, Jefferson, 1808–1889. 2. Statesmen—
United States—Biography. 3. Presidents—Confederate States of America—Biography. 4. Confederate States of America—Politics and government. 5. United States—History—Civil War,
1861–1865. I. Title.
    E467.1.D26C663 2009
    973.7'82092—dc22
    [B]
                                                                        2008010717

The paper in this book meets the guidelines for permanence and durability of the Committee on
Production Guidelines for Book Longevity of the Council on Library Resources. ∞

For Patricia

CONTENTS

JEFFERSON DAVIS AND THE CIVIL WAR ERA

INTRODUCTION

Jefferson Davis by William Cooper once again—one could legitimately ask why the need for a collection of essays on Davis from someone who not too long ago published a lengthy biography of him. I posed that same question to myself before deciding to proceed with this book. My answer was obviously yes; yes, this collection would serve a valid purpose.[1]

Each of these essays originated as a talk. Both before my biography appeared in 2000 and especially afterward, I have had the privilege of speaking before a number of audiences about different aspects of Jefferson Davis's life and career. Looking over these manuscripts, I realized certain of them concentrated on his relationship with critical topics of the Civil War era. Because of their sharp focus on central issues, I judged they illuminated Davis's role during those turbulent years.

Although my interpretation here of Davis and his involvement in these areas does not materially differ from the views expressed in *Jefferson Davis, American,* I do not see this book as repetitious. In the biography my assessments of Davis and major subjects such as the politics of secession or the Confederate war in the West run through various chapters. Here they are delineated in a few pages. In these essays a reader can readily obtain a perception of how Davis reacted to and dealt with a variety of important subjects throughout the Civil War era. At the same time, because each essay is self-contained, a bit of repetition occurs, especially at the beginning of several. I decided that maintaining the integrity of the individual discussions required some minimal iteration. In addition, the existence of *Jefferson Davis, American* has influenced my use of citations in this book. Because it treats context and details Davis's activities, here I concentrate my notes on quotations, acknowledging both my biography and other secondary sources where I think appropriate.

The essays between these covers range from the prewar period to the postwar years, with the majority concerned with the war. The first, and the only one previously published, examines Davis as an antebellum politician. The next looks closely at Davis's complex connection with secession. Then come six studies of Davis and the Confederate experience, with topics including states' rights, the politics of command and strategic decisions, the role of war leader, and the meaning of the war. The final item considers a little known event that points to Davis's key position in the formation of the Lost Cause ideology. These nine essays present distinct interpretations of Davis and consequential questions during the Civil War era.[2]

1

JEFFERSON DAVIS AND THE SUDDEN
DISAPPEARANCE OF SOUTHERN POLITICS

Before the Civil War, Jefferson Davis was a superlative politician. Such a claim smacks of heresy in the face of the legion of critics who have branded him as stiff-necked, unbending, doctrinaire, and overbearing. Jefferson Davis, either as an upright, dogmatic priest of principle or an inept, autocratic bureaucrat miscast in the role of politician, is a historical and historiographical staple.

That these robustly long-lived portrayals of Davis originated with both enemies and friends helps explain, perhaps, their seeming immortality. Characterizing Davis as cold, resentful, authoritarian, and despotic, Edward Pollard, an angry wartime opponent, summarized the views of Davis's antebellum and wartime foes. Pollard asserted that Davis's grievous faults caused the failure of his presidency and of the Confederate States of America. Although approaching Davis from a quite different perspective, Varina Davis, in her memoir of her husband published in 1890, added to this portrait of a man ill-suited for politics. She reported that he "did not know the arts of the politician and would not practice them if understood." What he really knew about, according to Mrs. Davis, was soldiering, and that was the path he really wanted to take.[1]

Historians, with few exceptions, have followed those leads. Bell

Wiley depicted a man who did not see the need for "cultivating the elementary art of political maneuver" and who certainly did not exhibit the attributes of "the master politician." In his mammoth history of sectional conflict and war, Allan Nevins found Davis's gifts sadly lacking, though he finally did inch toward the view that Davis did about as well as anyone else could have during his Confederate ordeal. In probably the most damning indictment of Davis as a political leader, David Potter not only proclaimed that his shortcomings doomed the Confederacy but also suggested that if Abraham Lincoln had been in Davis's place, the Confederacy might have succeeded.[2]

More recent students have not discovered a fundamentally new Jefferson Davis. In his stimulating *After Secession: Jefferson Davis and the Failure of Confederate Nationalism,* Paul Escott states bluntly that the president shouldered much of the responsibility for Confederate defeat. Moreover, Escott emphasizes that Davis's personal deficiencies were instrumental in causing the Confederate catastrophe. Likewise, in his path-breaking study of Confederate politics, George Rable finds Davis not up to the challenge, especially as a political leader. Rable argues that he lacked and was never able to develop crucial political talents essential for an effective president. A modern Davis biographer does not disagree. William C. Davis presents a president so unfit for national leadership and with a basic "contempt" for political arts that the reader can only come away amazed that any of Jefferson Davis's contemporaries could ever have considered him an appropriate choice for the highest public office in the fledgling country.[3]

Of course, Davis is almost always compared to Lincoln. One inescapable truth is that Lincoln's side won and Davis's lost. Only that fact, in Ludwell Johnson's mind, raises Lincoln above Davis. But Johnson has few fellow members in his "Davis is better than Lincoln" club. Those historians at all sympathetic with Davis in the comparison contest generally adopt Nevins's eventual position: He had ability and did the best he could, and probably no one could have done better, but still he was no match for Lincoln. Even so, this stance drives people to look for Davis's blemishes and inadequacies, for which the evidence apparently abounds.[4]

I have no intention here of challenging the overwhelmingly prevailing view of Davis's political delinquency as Confederate president. Rather, I will ask why it occurred. Although the scholars above have largely concentrated on the war years, they have concurred, either openly or tacitly, with Roy Nichols that the antebellum Davis had "already indicat[ed] that capacity for political failure which was to be amply demonstrated by him when he became President of the Confederacy." My contention is that the antebellum Davis was quite different from Nichols's political cripple and from the consensus interpretation of the Confederate Davis. And if the consensus view of the Confederate Davis is correct, then something dramatic had to have happened to make it so.[5]

Just a glance reveals Jefferson Davis's impressive antebellum political career. He started at the bottom with a failed run in 1843 for the Mississippi legislature. He moved to the winner's circle with his work as presidential elector in 1844 and remained there the next year when he was victorious in a statewide race for the U.S. House of Representatives. In the summer of 1846, he left the House to fight in the Mexican War. Returning a hero, he entered the U.S. Senate in 1847, and from then until January 1861 he sat either in the Senate or the cabinet for all but eighteen months. In the 1850s he was easily the most prominent political figure in Mississippi. That is surely an enviable political record, though strange for a man supposedly a hater of politics and the antithesis of a politician.

A closer look at Jefferson Davis and politics, at Davis as a politician, is in order. I want to make clear what I intend with the term *politician*. First, it implies participation in the political process, from indicating the initial ambition for office to campaigning to behaving like a person who likes and wants to continue in office. Second, and perhaps more important, I refer to a mindset that understands politics as a means toward an end. In the American political system of the mid-nineteenth century, that meant working through institutions and with other people to attain goals. This description might sound like a truism, but too often southern leaders like Davis are thought of as men who stood up and announced their principles, shunning the give-and-take of political intercourse while preaching their version of political truth. In this scenario such men rode alone like political knights searching for an ideological grail. Of course, every age has its quota of such Galahads, but Jefferson Davis before 1861 absolutely never belonged to that band.

When Jefferson Davis emerged in 1843 from an eight-year self-imposed seclusion following the death of his first wife, his ambition for public office was evident. His wealthy and influential older brother Joseph provided him with entree to the local Democratic party. Jefferson grasped his opportunity. With legislative elections approaching and facing problems with candidates, Warren County Democrats turned to an untested, untried planter in his mid-thirties. Davis readily agreed, even though he expected to lose because of the heavy Whig majority in the county. He made a hard run that included his willingly debating Mississippi's most prominent Whig, Seargent S. Prentiss. Despite his strenuous effort, he realized his expectation and lost.[6] Still, it is hard to imagine a better way for an aspiring political neophyte to garner favor from both party notables and party voters.

Therefore, no doubt remained about Davis's ambition for political preferment. Although in the style of his time he often asserted both that he longed for private life and that he would never put himself forward for office, his activities repeatedly belied such claims. Perhaps a senatorial antagonist exaggerated when he described Davis as "burning up with ambition." But considerable truth resides in Andrew Johnson's assessment. Davis's vigorously effective performance as a presidential elector in 1844 so impressed the party faithful that the next year the state Democratic convention nominated him to run for Congress. Despite debilitation from illness, Davis did not hesitate to commence a rigorous campaign trip, a determination that greatly worried his new wife of seven months.[7]

Political ambition was paramount for Jefferson Davis. After less than a year in the House of Representatives, he left for the Mexican War, a decision blended of ambition and patriotism. Once again he rejected the pleas of his young wife that he not go. A few years later he was quite blunt, declaring to her, "your claim on my time though first could my heart decide." But his heart did not command. Politics interfered. "Circumstances" have "pressed" me "immediately," he explained as he informed her that another five months would pass before they could see each other again.[8]

Davis knew that his political success required his personal attention. He was never out of touch with his political friends and operatives while in Mexico. Returning a hero, he eagerly embraced an appointment to the U.S. Senate. Within a few months of his taking his seat in December 1847, the legislature would decide whether to retain him. From Washington he let an associate know that he was more interested in the legislature's choice than if he had stayed in Mississippi, though admitting that he did not want to be recalled. Albert G. Brown, a major force in Mississippi politics and a man both envious and wary of Davis, testified to Davis's successful cultivation of his political field. He reported that at the state Democratic convention of 1855, "Davis was there directing affairs in person." And to good effect, for Brown lamented, "his friends got possession of the convention and managed every thing their own way."[9]

Davis was not at all reluctant to have his story and his views placed before the voting public. In his failed run for governor in 1851, a campaign biography prepared by a political ally presented him in the most favorable possible light. *A Sketch of the Life of Jefferson Davis, the Democratic Candidate for Governor* contained much personal information that could hardly have been made available without his knowledge. Then in 1858 *Harper's Weekly* published a supremely positive front-page profile complete with a large illustration of the Mississippian. Concerned about the political fallout from certain addresses on the sectional issue that he made in 1858, Davis agreed with advisers and brought out an edition of his speeches. And he worked hard to distribute it. Such exertions are certainly not what one would expect from a man who really wanted to return permanently to private life in Warren County.[10]

No other activity demonstrated more clearly Davis's determination to triumph as a politician than his unceasing speaking tours through his state. The Mississippi political arena of the 1840s and 1850s was home to a rowdy, rough-and-tumble spectator sport. White manhood suffrage had existed since 1832, and the sovereign voters required wooing and intermingling from prospective officeholders. This was emphatically not a political world in which rich planters sipping sherry and juleps in elegant drawing rooms controlled candidates and elections. Although energetic campaigning accompanied by constant speechmaking and "pressing the flesh" antedated Davis's entry into the arena, no diminution took place during his time there.

From the very beginning Jefferson Davis participated fully and willingly in the demanding ordeal set up by Mississippi voters for those who wanted their allegiance. Abominable roads, poor transportation, nasty weather, and uncertain accommodations notwithstanding, Davis and his compatriots made their required treks through towns, villages, and countryside. In his initial statewide campaign as a presidential elector in 1844, Davis gave at least sixteen speeches in eleven different counties. Possibly his wife overstated the case when she later claimed that before the campaign no more than a dozen men outside Warren County knew her husband's name. There is no doubt, however, that Davis's performance catapulted him toward the front rank of his party. The very next year, in his victorious race for Congress, he spoke in at least twelve counties. During 1851 as Mississippi debated fundamental issues resulting from the Compromise of 1850, Davis seemingly lived on the campaign trail. From early May to mid-June, he made twenty-four stops in central and northern Mississippi. From the end of June through mid-August, he mounted podiums some thirteen times from Natchez to Oxford.[11]

When he served for a second time in the U.S. Senate between 1857 and 1861, Davis did not alter this active, engaged pattern. He planned a tour through the upper half of Mississippi for the fall of 1857. In the presidential contest of 1860, he spent the final six weeks traveling and speaking throughout the state. But these oratorical journeys often left him physically spent. On several occasions exhaustion and illness forced him to delay or curtail his schedule. Never, however, did he jettison this essential, albeit physically debilitating, part of the Mississippi politician's life.[12]

Although Davis made sure that he often personally appeared among Mississippi voters, he also recognized that many of them expected tangible results from officeholders. He never let them down. Reporting to a constituent in December 1845 that he did not have the answer to a land problem, the new congressman continued, "not willing to delay any longer I write now to assure you that your case shall not be neglected." Davis used whatever tack he thought would be effective with the Washington bureaucracy to help his constituents. Attempting to get a midshipman's warrant in the U.S. Navy for a young Mississippian, Davis reminded the secretary of the navy that "we of Mississippi have less than our proportionate share of navy appointments." Sending government publications such as the surveys of possible transcontinental railroad routes and reports of the Patent Office to political friends, and at times even to opponents, kept him in touch with voters and imprinted his name on their minds. His diligent efforts on this front had the desired result. When "a common farmer," James B. Smith, who led "a humble life" thanked the senator for several publications, he identified Davis as the only member of the Mississippi congressional delegation who had "so far condescended from his high *pinnacle of Congressional Glory*, so as to favor me with anything of importance from Headquarters." Davis thereafter had a loyal champion.[13]

Jefferson Davis took a systematic approach to constituent service, a task to which he obviously attached considerable importance. When he returned to Washington as a senator in 1847, he could not locate certain books and papers he had left behind when he headed to Mexico in the summer of 1846. The ensuing problem, as he told a colleague back in Mississippi, was that he had no list of correspondents. To remedy this unacceptable situation, he asked his fellow Democrat to send him a roster of appropriate names. Senator Davis used a ledger to keep track of his political base. The ledger of more than four hundred pages, with around 80 percent filled, begins with a catalog of Mississippi newspapers by town and county. There is also a roll of correspondents, individual and institutional, again by town and county, with an alphabetically arranged table of contents.[14]

For Jefferson Davis, loyalty to the Democratic Party remained a touchstone through the antebellum years. When he began his political career as a legislative candidate, the Democratic newspaper in his county called him "a sterling democrat." Two years later during his race for Congress, that same newspaper described him as "a Democrat to the core." His party identity and loyalty never wavered. As late as 1860 he vigorously exerted himself to get the national Democratic convention to stay together and choose a nominee who could heal intraparty wounds and lead the party to victory.[15]

Davis's sense of political fealty underscored his bond to the Democratic Party. To a friend he wrote in 1851 "that my political life has been devoted to the democratic cause." In a campaign speech the following year, he identified himself as "a party man, [who] had been bred in the paths of Democracy, and had never deviated from them." Repeating those sentiments before the U.S. Senate in 1858, Davis declared that his "relations to the party are those of a common opinion and unity of principle." To the Mississippi Democratic Convention of 1859, he portrayed the party as "sacred to us as the cause of truth and of our country."[16]

Simultaneously the party had a profound call on Davis. He loved being in the Senate, yet he voluntarily left in 1851 for a considerably less attractive alternative, running for governor of Mississippi. His explanation for this action testified to the power of the party. "It was in accordance with that rule of conduct which required me as a democrat to serve my party where they require me, not where my taste or ambition might dictate."[17] Not even the most stalwart party man, not even James K. Polk, for example, could have come forth with a more ringing credo.

For Davis, however, party loyalty was not an end in itself. As he proclaimed in a public letter, "party consultation and party organization are the means, not the end." A party could be justified, in Davis's mind, by adherence to "principle alone."[18] To him the Democratic Party stood for his most cherished principles: strict construction of the Constitution and states' rights. Those two fundamental precepts had, of course, a variety of manifestations.

The presidential election of 1848 provides an apt perspective on Davis's view of party loyalty. In that year the Whig presidential nominee was Zachary Taylor, his first father-in-law, his former commanding general in Mexico, and his close friend. Personally Davis overwhelmingly preferred Taylor; in fact he had been involved in discussions aimed at making Taylor the Democratic standard bearer. But when he found his personal favorite wearing the wrong political uniform, Davis did not hesitate. In public speeches in Mississippi he affirmed his high regard for Taylor but declared emphatically that his creed meant his vote would go to the Democratic candidate. Privately he wrote that his affection for the man "will be opposed by my convictions, and adherence to measures."[19]

Protecting political principles did not mean for Davis the abandonment of practical politics. In the summer of 1846, he delayed leaving Washington to join his Mississippi regiment until the House had decided on tariff reduction. In this instance he showed that he was a skilled political trader as well as a party loyalist. In return for promising President Polk that he would remain in Congress until the crucial vote, Davis received the president's pledge that he would direct the secretary of war to fill all of Davis's requisitions promptly.[20]

Unlike the triumphant struggle over the Walker Tariff in 1846, Davis did not always end up on the winning side. Political defeat did not, however, alter his commitment to the basic behavior of political professionals of his time. He accepted the loss and moved on to fight another battle another day. This attitude was never clearer than in the contest over the Compromise of 1850. In the long months of angry debate over the compromise measures, Davis fought with all his skill and energy against the compromise; especially tenacious was his opposition to California statehood. But he could stop neither the admission of California nor the general success of the compromise. Toward the close of the struggle, he told the Senate that he knew the outcome and would no longer argue the merits of the bill.[21]

Although he had failed in the Senate, Davis returned home determined to get Mississippians to take a firm stand against the compromise. He insisted that approval of the compromise by Congress did not mean that Mississippi had obediently to accept it. He urged the state to denounce the compromise, but there he suffered one more licking when Mississippi refused to act as he thought best.[22]

Despite the losses in Washington and at home, he kept his faith. Davis publicly announced in 1851 that Mississippi's acceptance of the compromise required the same of him because he was "bound by every principle of his cherished democracy." A year later while regrouping, he informed a political confidant that reprisals against former enemies should never motivate their policy. Davis expressed "no purpose of revenge which will prevent me from acting with those who return to the standard of Democracy." He would even "cooperate with those who stabbed me."[23]

During the secession crisis, Jefferson Davis used all of his political skills to avert what he saw as an impending catastrophe. In the crucial two months between the election of Abraham Lincoln on November 6, 1860, and the secession of Mississippi on January 9, 1861, he never advocated disunion, though he did believe in the constitutional right of secession. His own convictions as well as the realities of Mississippi politics demanded from him a recital of the legality of secession.

Davis handled his professions deftly, however. He always powerfully proclaimed his devotion to the United States. In response to a fellow southerner telling the Senate in 1850 that the South was his country, Davis proudly exclaimed, "I, sir, am an American citizen." To those in the Senate who dared name him a disunionist, he riposted in "monosyllables." Seven years later in Mississippi, he denounced the "brainless intemperance of those who desire a dissolution of the Union, and who found in every rustling leaf fresh evidence of volcanic eruption." To another Mississippi audience in 1858, Davis made clear, "I love the flag of my country with more than filial affection."[24]

In addition to proclamations of devotion to the Union, Davis repeatedly argued that the situation of the South was not so desperate as to call for breaking up the Union. He took that approach during the heated months of 1850 and 1851 as well as later in the decade, when he informed the Mississippi legislature that circumstances did not warrant embracing secession, "the last alternative."[25] Even though he confronted mounting sectional extremism in Mississippi, his firm statement of principles coupled with denials that conditions called for their invocation permitted him to retain both his political base and his independence. All the while he struggled to postpone the need to turn principles into action.

Even the Republican triumph in 1860 did not change Davis's basic approach and stance. In the immediate aftermath of Lincoln's victory, he urged caution and care. Responding to a request for his opinion from the South Carolina fire-eater Robert Barnwell Rhett Jr., Davis refused to give his approval to immediate secession. He informed Rhett of his doubt that the Mississippi legislature would call a state convention or even select delegates to a possible South-wide meeting. He also pointed to the difficulties he foresaw for South Carolina should the Palmetto State act alone. Later in November the governor of Mississippi brought the state's congressional delegation together to discuss various alternatives in the crisis. Again cautioning against haste, Davis opposed any immediate and independent action by his state. In all probability he was somewhat surprised that a majority advocated prompt and direct action.[26]

When he reached Washington for the momentous second session of the Thirty-sixth Congress, he was still striving for some way to avoid disaster. Willing to work with almost anyone, he reached out in every direction, from the Democratic president James Buchanan, to the independent senator John J. Crittenden, to the Republican senator William Henry Seward, a personal friend of Davis despite their sharp partisan differences.[27] Although discouraged to do so, he agreed to serve on the Committee of Thirteen, charged by the Senate to search for a way to reconcile Republicans and southern Democrats. He certainly made known his willingness to accept the leading compromise proposal, the Crittenden Compromise, if the Republicans would only do so.[28]

He, the Committee of Thirteen, the Senate, and Congress all failed, of course. No solution was found, and the states of the Deep South began parading out of the Union. The failure to find a political formula that would preserve the Union struck Davis with terrible force. The Union was gone, and fratricidal war loomed.

Davis's emotional distress was palpable. What he defined as "unutterable grief" afflicted him. To his old comrade and former boss Franklin Pierce he wrote sadly, "now I come to the hard task of announcing to you that the hour is at hand which closes my connection with the United States, for the independence and Union of which my father bled and the service of which I have sought to imitate the example he set for my guidance." The next day Jefferson Davis made his final appearance in the Senate. After briefly defending Mississippi's decision to secede, he closed with memories of shared experiences and denials of any personal hostility. The response of his listeners reflected his own intense feelings.[29]

Those who knew Davis and witnessed his time of trial testified to the emotional and psychological agony that gripped him. A family friend who witnessed Davis's farewell from the Senate gallery reported that he "was firm and manly—but pale and evidently suffering." After his remarks Davis walked down Pennsylvania Avenue with two close companions. His anguish was obvious. Taking the hand of one, he declared to them, "dear friends this is the saddest day of my life." That night a Senate colleague remained with Davis and his wife until 3:00 A.M. Senator William Gwin remembered a "tortured" Davis.[30]

Davis emerged from the trauma of the secession winter with a sharply altered outlook. When he departed Washington on January 22, 1861, he left behind the politics he had known and practiced for almost two decades. The formation of the Confederate States of America and his selection as its first president less than three weeks later confirmed in his mind the different perspective from which he now would view politics. President Jefferson Davis considered himself the leader of a holy crusade that he identified with the American Revolution. He told his inaugural audience that together they were striving "to perpetuate the principles" of "our fathers." In his first message to Congress after Fort Sumter, he directly associated the South of 1861 with the American colonies of the 1770s. Both had been forced to break away from tyranny in order to preserve liberty.[31]

For Davis the world of politics had changed fundamentally. The new Confederate States of America was not the old United States of America. Just as a new country had been born, so a new politics had come into being. To guarantee the success of the Confederate experiment, old political ways had to be put aside. This attitude was not unique to Davis. Many southerners hoped for, even expected, a fresh political day.[32]

With Jefferson Davis, however, profound personal motivation propelled his fervent insistence on a new politics. From the painful loss of the old Union and his place in it, he forged a passionate commitment to the fledgling Confederacy. And this cause could not fail. Because traditional politics had not succeeded in saving the Union, it certainly could not be relied on to preserve the Confederacy. Davis always believed, and here he was surely right, that he gave all of himself to the Confederate mission. He also risked much because his responsibility was so massive. In his view he and the Confederate States of America were one. No longer a cotton planter and slaveowner, no longer a citizen of Mississippi, and no longer a public servant representing his state, he had become a Confederate. All else, from his property to his private concerns, had to be shunted aside (or at the least placed in storage) until Confederate triumph was assured. Davis convinced himself, albeit with some rationalization, that he had accomplished that storing. From everyone else involved in the Confederate enterprise, the South's president expected, even demanded, the same full measure of selfless devotion that he was absolutely sure characterized his Confederate contribution.

Awareness of this mindset is essential to comprehend Davis's approach to his presidential task. The posture only stiffened with time. The trials and difficulties of leading his country through an increasingly horrible war brought forth an even greater sense of dedication. Their list is legion—the unending criticism, which grew shriller as

Confederate fortunes faded; the growing burden of military reverses with their numbing casualty totals; the piercing personal losses, including his and his revered brother Joseph's plantations being overrun by Union soldiers, which forced the septuagenarian Joseph to become a wandering refugee; and most awful, his cherished five-year-old son's accidental death at his Richmond home. His enhanced devotion ensured that Davis would be even more convinced of the rightness of his ways.

Politics did exist but only on the surface. In the initial cabinet organized in Montgomery, each state was allotted a seat. Bowing to implacable congressional pressure, Davis in 1862 removed Judah P. Benjamin from the War Department. Davis's Confederate political practice was not, however, one in which good men could seriously disagree or anyone could seemingly applaud himself. Davis too often confused agreement with him with devotion to duty. Disagreement or questioning or any hint of egotism became for him a challenge to the cause, a sign of limited commitment, a signal that personal interest was primary. Individuals who disagreed, questioned, or boasted did not deserve friendly, forbearing handshakes, wooing, or persuasion. Instead they merited brusqueness, chastisement, and belittlement.

In the Confederacy the old politician Davis was largely absent. In late 1847 political associates in Mississippi asked the then-senator to join them in a scheme to push aside one of his rivals, a man he roundly disliked. Refusing, Davis replied that his "notions of propriety" would not permit his interference. That Jefferson Davis did not become president of the Confederacy. Just over a decade later in 1858, bitter words by Davis in the Senate prompted a challenge from Judah P. Benjamin. When apprised by a mutual friend of Benjamin's reaction, Davis without pause announced: "I will make this all right at once. I have been wholly wrong." Then on the floor of the Senate, he publicly apologized, "I cannot gainsay . . . that my manner implied more than my heart meant." To his fellow senators he confessed, "I always feel pained, nay, more, I feel humiliated, when I am in a personal controversy with anybody." That Jefferson Davis did not work in Richmond between 1861 and 1865.[33]

The politician who had mastered Mississippi and who had attained great influence in the U.S. Senate did not transfer to the Confederate States of America. Jettisoning politics for a holy calling, Jefferson Davis wounded himself and his cause, perhaps fatally.

2

JEFFERSON DAVIS AND THE
POLITICS OF SECESSION

Because Jefferson Davis is best known as president of the Confederacy, most people assume that he advocated secession and that he played a leading role in breaking up the Union. These assumptions are simply wrong. Some historians have recognized that Davis was not a fire-eater, the term often used for those who preached secession and actively campaigned to destroy the Union, but still many of these scholars identify him as an extremist on sectional questions, especially slavery in the territories, which became the one insoluble issue in the crisis of the Union. According to their view, Davis's commitment to extremism bound and shackled him, causing him to approach the issue as an ideologue, not a politician.[1]

But here I will posit a different view. Without doubt Davis believed in the constitutional right of secession, yet he had a profound devotion to the Union. Moreover, he never considered the southern situation sufficiently perilous to warrant Mississippi's exercising her constitutional prerogative of secession. In addition, his perception of the South's position in the Union changed between 1850 and 1860. In Davis's mind these two issues—the place of the South in the Union and the question of secession—were inseparable.

With his belief in the constitutionality of secession, Davis heeded the states' rights interpretation of the Constitution widely accepted in the South before 1861. Initially formulated by Thomas Jefferson and James Madison in the 1790s and pushed even further by John C. Calhoun in the 1820s and 1830s, this exposition argued that the states, through their ratifying conventions, created the Constitution and thus the federal government. The states, the creators, were sovereign, not the federal government, the created. Carried to its logical conclusion, this thesis maintained that just as states had decided individually to come into the Union, each could individually decide to leave it. But for Davis secession was never the preferred action; he stressed that it should only occur "as the last remedy, the final alternative."[2]

Assessing the place of the South, Davis operated from two fundamental bases. To him, as to most other southerners before 1861, the Constitution guaranteed southerners as Americans equality in the nation. Davis also accepted Calhoun's position that only the possession of political power by the South ensured that equality. By the time that the Mississippian became an influential political figure in the late 1840s, southerners viewed that equality grounded in the U.S. Senate. There were fifteen free states and fifteen slave states in the Union; each group had thirty senators. By this time faster population growth in the North had already made that section dominant in the House of Representatives.

Davis burst on the national scene as a war hero after his exploits in Mexico in 1846 and 1847. Upon his return to Mississippi in mid-1847, he had to decide between two attractive offers. The governor of Mississippi offered him a vacant seat in the U.S. Senate, while the president of the United States offered to make him a brigadier general in the U.S. Army. In making his decision to appoint Davis a general, President James K. Polk underscored Davis's public standing. Polk found "public sentiment" clamoring for Davis; he decided that to keep Mississippi a Democratic state, he had "to yield" to that opinion. Choosing the Senate over the army, Davis arrived in Washington in November 1847 as an enormously popular military hero who had rapidly ascended to the highest level of Mississippi politics.[3]

The first major political issue the new senator confronted had to do with equality in both senses: the South in the nation and southerners as Americans. He concentrated on the territories, American lands not yet admitted as states; his focus would remain there until the Union came apart. The points at issue in 1847 and 1848 were the Oregon Territory and, more importantly, the Mexican Cession, the area that came to the United States after the Mexican War: the modern Southwest, with the jewel of California. The specific question that absorbed the attention of so many, including Davis, was slavery. Would slavery be permitted in those territories? The answer was so critical because it defined the American future. From its founding, the United States had been both slave and free. Westward expansion had been marked by slave and free states marching together to the Mississippi River and beyond. This debate had exploded a generation earlier over slavery in the Louisiana Purchase, which had been settled by the Missouri Compromise of 1820. As part of that agreement, a line was drawn all the way from the Mississippi River to the Rocky Mountains separating slavery from freedom. Both would continue to exist side by side.

Between 1847 and 1850, three major responses dominated deliberation in the nation and particularly in Congress. The first proposed to ban slavery in any territory. This proposition became known as "free soil." Even before the end of the Mexican War, its adherents had pushed for a measure that would mandate congressional prohibition of slavery anywhere in the Mexican Cession; this was the Wilmot Proviso, named for Pennsylvania congressman David Wilmot, who first introduced it in the House in 1846. In the late 1840s the measure passed the House of Representatives on a sectional vote, but the Senate always blocked it. In fact, before 1860 the Wilmot Proviso never won congressional approval.[4]

Davis saw the drive for free soil as politically motivated, an attempt by the North to dominate the Union and in so doing to subjugate the South. For him all the free-soil furor had one goal: "political strife for sectional supremacy." Its very notion that slavery blemished the nation requiring its banishment from the future appalled and even angered him. Davis told the Senate that the South can never "consent to be a marked caste, doomed, in the progress of national growth, to be dwarfed into helplessness and political dependence."[5]

Finally, his reaction was quite personal. Davis had been in combat in Mexico; he had even suffered a wound that still hobbled him. He was proud of his service. "I, sir, am an American citizen," he declared, and the United States is "my country." With emotion, he embraced his fellow veterans from slave states, asking, "Shall the widow and orphan of him who died in his country's quarrel, be excluded from the acquisition obtained in part by his blood?" His answer was a resounding no.[6]

For his own stand on the territories, Davis accepted what became the orthodox southern position, the second major response. Congress could not prohibit slavery in the national domain because slaveowners were citizens who had the constitutional right to take their property into territory belonging to all Americans. On this question John C. Calhoun forcefully articulated the feelings of southerners in no uncertain terms: "What then do we insist on is, not to extend slavery, but that we shall not be prohibited from immigrating with our property, in the territories of the United States, because we are slave-holders, or, in other words, we shall not on that account be disfranchised of a privilege possessed by all others, citizens and foreigners, without discrimination as to character, profession, or color. All, whether savage, barbarian, or civilized, may freely enter and remain, we only being excluded."[7]

While Davis totally agreed with Calhoun, he was quite willing to search for a political solution that would deviate from Calhoun's declaration. In other words Davis would bend. In the Senate in 1848, he voted with the majority on two compromise measures: one would extend the Missouri Compromise line to the Pacific Ocean, while the other would give federal courts jurisdiction over slavery in the territories. Both failed in the House. Compromise for Davis did not mean abandoning principle. Rather, in his view "to compromise is to waive the application, not to surrender the principle on which a right rests, and surely give no claim to further concession." On what was to him an absolutely crucial issue, he showed flexibility and a willingness to make a political deal.[8]

The third important reaction to the territorial crisis would take the question out of Congress. Under the rubric of popular sovereignty, this plan would turn over the decision on slavery to the people who actually lived in the territories. In short, this would make slavery in the territories a local issue, not a national one. It had the attractiveness of removing a volatile, seemingly intractable issue from the visible forum of Congress. Additionally it left conveniently vague the time at which the inhabitants of a territory could decide about slavery. As a result that date could be assigned according to the political wishes or needs of various adherents. At this time Davis opposed popular sovereignty, and he never liked it. In his mind the doctrine gave up the principle that southerners had the constitutional right to carry slave property into the common territory. But later he would lend his support to making popular sovereignty part of the Democratic Party's creed.

Between 1847 and 1849 none of these three positions commanded a majority in Congress. Thus the vast Mexican Cession remained unorganized. But this lack of official government organization became intolerable with the discovery of gold in California in 1849. The resulting flood of immigrants made organization essential.

When the first session of the Thirty-first Congress convened in December 1849, it faced a mountainous political problem. There is neither space nor need here to go into detail on the legislative history of what became known as the Compromise of 1850. A number of issues were involved as Congress tried to formulate a workable solution, but for Jefferson Davis one concern stood foremost—California. Men who often times agreed on little else made a great push to admit California as a state immediately. Many found this project attractive because all parties, even Calhoun, agreed that a state could make its own decisions on slavery; thus the prompt admission of California could finesse the fractious territorial issue. Everyone recognized that because of the makeup of its population at the time, California would join the Union as a free state.

Davis, along with other southerners, mostly Democrats, fought bitterly against California statehood. They argued that admitting California immediately, without any territorial phase, was an exception to the policy that had previously governed the admission of new states since the original thirteen. All others, they correctly maintained, had been either part of other states or territories, except for Texas, which had been an independent country. According to these opponents, the exception for California had but one goal, to hurt the South because southerners would have no opportunity to emigrate with their slaves. More importantly for Davis and his associates, a free California would upset the balance of state representation in the Senate. California statehood would result in sixteen free states and thirty-two senators to fifteen slave states and thirty senators. The result of that imbalance, Davis believed, would mirror what had already occurred in the House, a northern-dominated chamber that had passed the Wilmot Proviso and blocked the extension of the Missouri Compromise line.

Underscoring Davis's motive was his conviction that power derived from equality. The Mississippian struggled against the California bill to the very end. He failed, he said, not "for want of will, but for want of power." With feeling so strong that he wanted to act physically, to tear up the bill on the floor of the Senate, Davis nevertheless could not round up sufficient support. The great ripping never took place.[9]

Despite Davis's arduous efforts, the California bill passed through Congress in September 1850 as part of a series of measures that made up the Compromise of 1850. A major reason for the success of this compromise was the legislative skill of Senator Stephen A. Douglas of Illinois, a member of Davis's party. A political dynamo who shaped the successful legislative strategy, Douglas would reappear in Davis's future. Even though the compromise had been enacted, the Mississippian did not cease opposing it. All along he had insisted that the South had fundamental rights at stake, and if deprived of them, the South must act.

With the adjournment of Congress, Davis took his crusade against California and the compromise back to Mississippi. Yet for all his declaiming about violation of rights and danger to the South, his prescription for remedy never became specific. While he defined secession as a "catastrophe we will sincerely deplore," he also placed "responsibility" upon the supporters of the compromise, who in his judgment "have undermined the foundation on which the Union was erected." At the same time, he applauded the "historical association and national pride" that kept the Union whole. This along with the "social links" that tied together families even at "extreme ends of the Union" he described as "magic power."[10]

Although he wanted Mississippi officially to register displeasure, Davis did not spell out what form that registration might take, other than words of opposition. Despite his vagueness, two points are absolutely clear. He never embraced the Compromise of 1850 as a political good as did a majority in both his state and the South in general. Also, he never advocated secession as some did in Mississippi and in other southern states, especially South Carolina.

Davis ended up on the losing side in Mississippi, where the compromise deranged both parties. Pro-compromise forces, including a majority of Whigs and a minority of Democrats, formed the Union Party. On the other side a majority of Democrats allied with a minority of Whigs to create what they called the State-Rights Democratic Party. Outright secessionists were in the State-Rights Democratic ranks, but Davis was not one of them; yet he was tainted by their presence. As the gubernatorial candidate of his new party in 1851, he never managed to remove entirely the disunion stigma. The Union Party swept to victory and handed him an embarrassing political loss, the only one he knew between his election to Congress in 1845 and 1860.

This personal defeat matched the political reverse Davis believed the compromise had handed the South, but neither had the result he expected. He did not sit for long on the political sidelines. In 1853 the new Democratic president, Franklin Pierce, appointed Davis to the cabinet as secretary of war. Also, no signs emerged that the admission of California had generated a northern stampede over southern rights. In contrast the next half-dozen years persuaded Davis that he and the South had a secure place in the Union and that most northerners considered southerners good Americans. A man with his conviction could still hold high office, and the South retained ample political power. Thus his great worries of the late 1840s and the early 1850s were for naught. Even the rise of the Republican Party, with its anti-South rhetoric and cry for free soil, did not alter Davis's opinion. There were four major reasons for his optimism: his service with Pierce; the administration of James Buchanan; the Dred Scott decision of 1857; and his 1858 sojourn in Maine.

As secretary of war, Davis became an immensely influential member of the Pierce administration and a close friend of the president. That Pierce, from New Hampshire, and cabinet colleagues from New York, Massachusetts, Pennsylvania, and Indiana supported southern interests impressed Davis. The administration also backed specific southern demands. Most important, Pierce put the force of his office behind the effort to repeal the Missouri Compromise. With Davis acting as an important agent bringing together Stephen Douglas and the president for a critical meeting, the Democratic Party and the Pierce administration put their imprimatur on the Kansas-Nebraska Act of 1854, which opened the possibility of slavery in territory that had been closed to the institution by the Missouri Compromise.

Pierce's successor in the White House, James Buchanan of Pennsylvania, was another northern Democrat with strong southern proclivities. When Buchanan became president in 1857, Davis returned to the Senate but remained a close presidential advisor. Moreover, southerners dominated the new cabinet. In addition, the administration supported the South on the territorial issue, chiefly in a horribly mangled attempt to make Kansas a slave state. Not only did the Lecompton Constitution, which would have accomplished that goal, fail in Congress, but it also led to a fateful rupture in 1858 between Buchanan and southern Democrats on one side and the most popular northern Democrat, Senator Douglas, on the other when the latter refused to embrace Lecompton. Detestation replaced harmony with ill portents for the party, southern power, and the Union.

In March 1857, at the onset of Buchanan's presidency, the U.S. Supreme Court decided the Dred Scott case. In its ruling the court went far beyond deciding whether Dred Scott, a Missouri slave, was no longer enslaved because he had resided in free territory and a free state with his master, an army surgeon. While declaring Scott still a slave the court also ruled that Congress had no power to prohibit slavery in any territory. Furthermore, it even denied that blacks could be citizens. In holding against congressional prohibition, the court took its stand where most southerners, including Jefferson Davis, stood. Following Calhoun's assertions, legions of southerners maintained that as constitutionally protected property, slavery could not be banned from the national domain. In Davis's view Dred Scott gave the South the constitutional high ground. As he saw it, the Republican Party, with congressional prohibition its central tenet, had had its constitutional props knocked away. He was confident that in any territorial test case, a federal court would uphold the rights of slaveholders.

Additionally, a personal experience boosted Davis's conviction about the safety of the South in the Union. In the summer and fall of 1858, he spent several months in Maine recuperating from a serious illness. The warmth of his reception delighted and surprised the Mississippian. As he traveled through the state, he made several speeches, which generated a positive response. When he spoke he praised the Union and asserted that the North and South shared a common history and interlocking interests.

Davis rejoiced in the "common sense of nationality beat[ing] in every bosom." If Maine were ever in danger, he declared that Mississippi would rush to her rescue. In turn he was confident that Maine would do the same for Mississippi. Denouncing those he termed "trifling politicians" trying to divide the country, he employed a farmer's metaphor: "they are like the mosquitoes around the ox; they annoy, but they cannot wound, and never kill."[11]

Thus Davis saw North and South together. He did not perceive the North perpetrating an all-out assault on the South. In his view the South had on its side northern friends, political power, and the

Constitution. And not unimportant to an ambitious politician, Jefferson Davis was listened to not only in Mississippi but also in Washington and even Maine.

While still in Maine savoring his unexpected personal triumph, Davis was ambushed. He expected attacks from Republicans and some northern Democrats, even from a few southerners outside the Democratic Party, but he certainly did not anticipate assault from other southern Democrats. But they are exactly who struck him, men carrying the same states'-rights banner he so proudly upheld. Word came to him from allies in Mississippi that he was facing criticism in his own state and elsewhere in the South. Why? Rumors were circulating that Davis had declared the Union inviolable, which if true meant that secession would be unconstitutional. Davis hurried to deny this accusation. Truthfully he responded that he had praised the Union but had never denied the right of secession.

These denials did not, however, quiet the furor concentrated among the extreme southern-rights men, who operated on Davis's sectional left. In condemnation an Alabama editor described him as "a pitiable spectacle of human weakness and political equivocation." In Mississippi his arch-rival and fellow U.S. senator, Albert G. Brown, strove to best Davis as a defender of the South by staking out extreme political ground. Depicting a rapacious North determined to destroy slavery at all costs, Brown set up a simple choice for the South: give up either slavery or the Union. He claimed it was "madness" for anyone to think the onrushing tide of abolition could be halted or turned back. A number of Democratic newspapers in the state supported Brown, though the leading one, the *Jackson Mississippian*, remained stalwart for Davis. Bemused by the Democratic division, anti-Democrats in the state noted Brown's efforts to make political capital at Davis's expense. One of their major papers found hilarity in the intraparty political combat: "As Jeff. Davis goes North, Brown comes South. . . . Davis goes to Portland and Brown goes to the equator," chortled the editor. "If Davis should penetrate further into Maine, we shall probably hear of Brown bathing in the crater of a volcano."[12]

On the defensive, Davis fought back. He realized that his base and his prominence in Mississippi were at stake. Davis wrote public letters, made speeches, and finally at the request of supporters put out a brief volume of his speeches, chiefly those made in New England in 1858. His dedication provided the key to his efforts: "I have been induced by the persistent misrepresentation of popular addresses made by me at the North during 1858 to collect them . . . to present the whole . . . to the end that the case may be fairly before those whose judgment I am willing to stand of fall."[13]

Even while working to secure his standing in Mississippi, Davis also strove to find a middle way on the territorial issue between southern fire-eaters like Brown, who were crying for a slave code for the territories (that is, that Congress should do for the territories what individual slave states did within their borders), and northern Democrats unalterably opposed to a congressional slave code. In short, he hoped to unify his party on the most contentious question of the day.

Davis did make a proposal for the territories, though not a slave code, which most historians claim he made. In fact he deemed such a code unnecessary; moreover, he did not believe it could get through Congress. He worried about "over action by our friends," cautioning southerners not to push for too much. Davis simply wanted a statement of principle based on Dred Scott that stipulated that slaveholders had the right to take their slave property into the territories. He wanted no action. At the same time, Stephen Douglas asserted that no matter what the Dred Scott decision held, if local (territorial) legislation did not protect the institution, then the ruling was useless. There was a crucial difference between Douglas and Davis, however—Davis emphasized the constitutional point, which Douglas basically disregarded. The Senate in 1860 did pass Davis's resolution, but he never managed to have his plan viewed as the moderate measure around which, as he saw it, all good, patriotic citizens could rally. Both the fire-eaters like Brown and Douglas rejected Davis's proposition—the former because they wanted no settlement, the latter because he recognized that it could co-opt him and upset his presidential ambitions.[14]

While Davis's hopes on the territorial question did not materialize, he also found it impossible to implement his strategy for his party in 1860. He wanted Douglas pushed aside; too many southerners, Jefferson Davis included, distrusted him. Yet at the same time they considered a northerner essential as the party's presidential nominee. Davis desired a noncontroversial northern candidate and no specific platform, just a vague call for the Union and patriotism, rightly fearing that the party could not agree on a platform anyway. But Davis's hopes were shattered in the Democratic convention of 1860. Both the southern extremists and the Douglas men rejected his scenario. The convention came apart over both platform and candidate. Attempts to restore party unity failed. Eventually the Democrats fielded two candidates, one northern, Douglas, and one southern, Vice President John C. Breckinridge of Kentucky. As a seasoned professional politician, Davis realized that this division probably meant a Republican victory.

In the political storms of the late 1850s and 1860, Davis kept himself dominant in Mississippi, but he failed to find for his party a national middle way. All the while the political rhetoric in the Deep South was becoming bolder and more strident in anticipation of a possible Republican victory in the presidential election. The Mississippi Democratic Convention of 1859 even termed that outcome in and of itself a hostile act toward the South.

Davis himself had uttered similar remarks. After all, he had to protect himself in Mississippi, where Brown and his forces were always alert for anything they could brand as Davis's softness on slavery or the sectional question. He had declared that he would feel "disgraced by living under an abolition government." Under an abolitionist president, he told Mississippians, "you will become subjects of a hostile government." In the heat of a political speech Davis could match the extremists. Campaigning in Vicksburg in 1860, he proclaimed that if Mississippi resisted a Republican administration, he would be with her. "I will plant [her flag] upon the crest of battle and gathering around me Mississippi's best and bravest, will welcome the invader to the harvest of death; and future generations will point to a small hillock upon our border, which will tell the reception with which the invader met upon our soil."[15]

Yet Davis usually quickly inserted caveats in any remarks about the election of 1860 and what the South should do if a Republican were elected. At times he would substitute "abolitionist" for "Republican"; noting that all Republicans were not abolitionists, he said it would depend on the person. On the Senate floor he denied having ever said that the election of a Republican would require secession. Secession would occur only if the Republican president would not govern according to the Constitution "but pervert it to [the South's] destruction." At a rally in Mississippi in 1860, he was asked directly if the election of Abraham Lincoln would justify secession. Davis answered yes if, but only if, it were determined that Lincoln really was a black Republican, or abolitionist. He kept trying to leave at least a crack in his secessionist rhetoric.[16]

In early November came the news Davis had been both expecting and dreading, Lincoln's election as president. Yet the senator did not rush to join the secession bandwagon. In fact he tried to slow it down. Responding to an inquiry from a South Carolina fire-eater, Davis said that Mississippi would not secede alone. Furthermore, he told his correspondent that South Carolina should wait to see what the South would do, not rush out on its own. When the governor of his state called a meeting in Jackson of the congressional delegation to consult on the proper reaction to Lincoln's victory, Davis urged caution. But he alone counseled against immediate action. Before these deliberations concluded, Davis received a telegram urging him to come promptly to Washington. He left Jackson but informed his associates that he would be governed by their decision.[17]

Davis desperately hoped for some kind of deal in Congress between southern Democrats and Republicans that would hold the Union together. In the frantic month of December 1860, his hopes rose and fell. By mid-month he had given up on the Union, signing a statement proclaiming, "the argument is exhausted." But on the twenty-first he agreed to serve on a special Senate committee of thirteen, charged to find a settlement to the crisis.[18]

The major proposal before the Senate and the committee was known as the Crittenden Compromise, named for its sponsor John. J. Crittenden, senator from Kentucky and one-time protégé of Henry Clay, the great compromiser. The key feature of the Crittenden Compromise would extend the Missouri Compromise line westward through the Mexican Cession, leaving California intact. Davis, along with the other Democrats on the committee, signaled their acceptance of the proposal provided that Republicans did also. But all five Republicans united in refusing to do so. Recognizing its failure, the committee at the end of the month reported to the Senate that it could not agree on Crittenden or any other compromise measure.

At this point Davis gave up. "My hope of an honorable peaceable settlement was not abandoned until the report of the Com.," he wrote a few years later. He then joined in conversations concerning a new southern government, though without elation. Reluctantly he let the Union go. Davis remained in Washington until he received official notice of Mississippi's secession on January 19, 1861. Two days later he gave his farewell to the Senate. To a friend he called it "the saddest day of my life."[19]

3

JEFFERSON DAVIS AND STATES' RIGHTS IN THE CONFEDERACY

States' rights and its influence on the Confederate States of America is a staple of southern history. Perhaps its most famous, and in some ways most lasting, formulation came in 1925 when historian Frank L. Owsley penned his famous epitaph for the Confederacy—"Died of State Rights." Jefferson Davis, as Confederate president, was certainly at the center of this issue, especially the extent to which he promoted the doctrine in the South or jettisoned it in favor of centralized power during a time of war. Two distinct, though closely related, questions more pointedly focus the discussion on Davis's role in promoting or retarding states' rights. First, did a sharp difference on states' rights exist between the antebellum and the Confederate Davis? Second, did Davis and the issue of states' rights have significant sway on the course of Confederate history?[1]

Davis is generally depicted as a steadfast states' righter, in my judgment correctly so. Early in his political career, he identified with what legions of southerners regarded as the orthodox states' rights doctrine formulated by Thomas Jefferson and James Madison and given political expression in the Virginia and Kentucky Resolutions of 1798 and 1799. In fact Davis absorbed the ideological testament even before his political career began, for he identified himself as a Democrat and follower of Andrew Jackson, who in Davis's mind had revitalized the old Jeffersonian party. He also proudly professed loyalty to the ideas of the leading states' rights spokesman of his day, John C. Calhoun. Of course, by the 1830s Jackson and Calhoun had become political enemies, but Davis never acknowledged their falling out, maintaining his twin loyalty.

As a newly elected congressman, Davis proved his doctrinal orthodoxy by opposing even the venerated Calhoun on a constitutional issue. In his quest to unite the South and the West, and to further his own presidential ambitions, Calhoun in the mid-1840s came up with the idea of the "inland sea." He used this inventive approach to get around the traditional states' rights opposition to internal improvements, federal expenditures for state and local projects usually connected with transportation. In this scheme the South Carolinian designated the Mississippi River and its major tributaries as the "inland sea." In this guise federal expenditures could pass states' rights muster, for all agreed that the national government could support coastal improvements such as lighthouses and harbors.[2]

Addressing the House in 1846, Davis announced that he could not go along with Calhoun's stance. He repeated the pure states' rights gospel that decreed that the Constitution had to be strictly constructed and that Congress only possessed the powers specifically granted to it in the written Constitution. "To all which has been said of the inherent powers of the Government, I answer, it is the creature of the States." Thus according to Davis, the federal government "could have no inherent power, all it preserves was delegated by the States, and it is therefore that our Constitution is not an instrument of limitations, but of grants."[3]

All through the 1850s Davis adhered to his oft-stated belief that states' rights, the inherent power residing in the individual states, remained at the core of the Constitution and American liberty. To a Mississippi audience in 1858, he made absolutely clear his view: "I would cling tenaciously to our constitutional Government, seeing as I do in the fraternal Union of equal States." Speaking before the Senate for the final time in January 1861, Davis defended secession as "an essential attribute of State sovereignty."[4]

Yet there was one huge caveat in Davis's devotion to states' rights: national defense, or what today we would call national security. In this area he did not hold to a strict ideological position. In fact in this matter he found himself in Calhoun's spot with his "inland sea," with states' rights purists faulting him. The key issue was a transcontinental railroad. As secretary of war from 1853 to 1857, Davis had responsibility for the military defense of the country. By this time, of course, the United States had become a continental nation. The Oregon Territory had been organized in 1849 and California admitted as a state a year later.

As secretary of war, Davis worried about the potential menace to the Pacific Coast of a foreign maritime power, for example, Great Britain. Combating a threat on that coast with forces from the eastern seaboard required a lengthy transit: either by sea to Central America, then overland to the Pacific, and again by sea up to California; or by sea all the way around Cape Horn at the tip of South America. In Davis's opinion such an incredibly long supply line made defending the West Coast basically impossible. Moreover, he faced the ever-increasing problem of protecting the growing number of American settlers heading across the plains toward the Rocky Mountains. Attempting to cope with these assignments, the U.S. Army confronted tremendous logistical and operational difficulties.

Secretary Davis thought a transcontinental railroad the only real answer to this problem. Until one could be built, though, he turned to various stopgaps like the famous camel experiment. In this venture Davis intended to use camels in the southwestern desert for transportation and fighting. Convinced by Turkish and French examples, he believed employing these desert-friendly animals in place of horses and mules would give American soldiers an advantage in the vast arid landscape stretching westward from central Texas. Indeed, initial trials proved promising. But for Davis this initiative was only temporary.

He wanted a railroad to the Pacific, and he urged Congress to authorize its construction. Even more, he advocated that the U.S.

government build it. In doing so he perceived no constitutional difficulty. First and foremost, he pointed out that the Constitution had delegated (a favorite word of strict constructionists) to the federal government the duty of defending the nation. He went on to say that the government owned the territory and the railroads would be constructed mostly on federal land, chiefly for military purposes.[5]

But during his years as war secretary, Davis's hopes for a government-built railroad never materialized. States' rights opponents, chiefly southerners, attacked the proposal, using language that Davis had used against Calhoun's propositions for the Mississippi Valley. Then the political problem of an eastern terminus caused gridlock. All assumed there would be only one route, and southerners and northerners were determined that their section would win the prize.

When Davis returned to the Senate in 1857, he continued to press for the railroad, utilizing the same arguments. To overcome constitutional and political problems, he and others suggested contracting with private companies, using public lands and government loans to pay the cost, but this proved futile. Once more, southern states' rights purists fought against the senator and the railroad. But for Jefferson Davis the needs of national defense overrode the niceties of states' rights constitutionalism. Ultimately constitutional objections and sectional politics stymied railroad proponents—no transcontinental railroad was built before the Civil War.[6]

The creation of the Confederate States of America in 1861 did not end the states' rights debate. The founders of the new country made states' rights a fundamental building stone of their constitution. The preamble spoke of "each State acting in its sovereign and independent character." Davis certainly did not oppose such emphasis. At the outset of his administration, he utilized the same states' rights language he had long employed in Washington and Mississippi. In his inaugural as provisional president, he noted that "sovereign States" made up the Confederacy. That same phrase appeared in his message to the special session of the Confederate Congress he called after Fort Sumter.[7]

But issues of national defense quickly came to the fore. The firing on Fort Sumter and the outbreak of war occurred only two months after Davis had taken office as provisional president. The government, still under construction, quickly moved to a war footing. From the outset Davis foresaw a long, tough struggle. For example, he urged Congress to authorize enlistments in the army for the duration of the conflict, or at least three years. Yet he was only able to get authorization for one-year enlistments from a Congress that preferred six months.

Still, Davis did not simply jettison his long-term allegiance to the holy writ of states' rights. In an address to the Army of Tennessee in October 1863, he proclaimed that the Confederacy had been "forced to take up arms to vindicate the political rights, the freedom, equality, and State sovereignty which were the heritage purchased by the blood of your revolutionary sires." As late as the fall of 1864, in a circular letter to six governors, he remained quite cognizant of the rights of states.[8]

At the same time, however, the course of the war shaped his sense of duty and his view of appropriate public policy. In the spring of 1862, fearing the decimation of Confederate ranks with the expiration of twelve-month enlistments, he proposed the first national conscription law in American history. Prompt attacks on conscription as an unconstitutional aggrandizement of power by the central government poured forth. One of the most notable assaults came from Georgia's governor, Joseph Brown, who claimed that Congress could call the state militias to suppress invasion and also provide for organizing and disciplining those units. The constitutional power of the central government to raise and maintain armies stopped there. For Brown, Davis's proposal violated the constitution in a naked power grab.

Responding, the president averred that the constitution made the central government responsible for national defense; specifically it authorized Congress to organize and maintain armies. In sum, Davis argued as he had as a U.S. cabinet officer and senator in the 1850s: national defense required national action. As he read the United States and the Confederate States constitutions, both gave the central government the duty to defend the nation. Each unambiguously granted power to Congress to raise and maintain armies. Thus in his mind, conscription easily passed the constitutional test. Davis made similar arguments about instituting impressment and suppressing habeas corpus. Yet his case never convinced Brown and others like him who described Davis as a power-mad despot determined to augment national authority and in so doing destroy what had been fundamental at the birth of the Confederacy, states' rights.[9]

This essay is not the place for a lengthy discussion of Confederate politics, but I do want to make some general comments. In his pathbreaking book on Confederate politics, *The Confederate Republic*, George Rable correctly avoids placing states' rights at the center of debate. He instead offers "the politics of national unity" versus "the politics of liberty" as the fault line dividing Confederates politically. This formulation is both thoughtful and legitimate. For those committed to the "politics of national unity," Confederate independence stood as the key goal. In the name of national independence, they would support legislative initiatives such as conscription as well as the growth of executive power. In contrast, the followers of "the politics of liberty" interpreted laws like conscription and increasing executive authority as dangerous threats to fundamental rights and liberties. These men often expressed their views in the language of states' rights, arguing that consolidation of national and executive power threatened the destruction of liberty best protected by the individual states.[10]

Fitting Davis neatly into one of these two patterns is problematical, however. He was absolutely committed to national unity, supporting a number of measures making both the central government in general and the executive in particular more powerful. Yet in his mind such powers had but one end, protecting Confederate liberty, the liberty both of the country and of its citizens. He made that point time and time again. Davis's message to Congress in December 1863 approached eloquence: "Whatever obstinacy may be displayed by the enemy in his desperate sacrifice of money, life, and liberty in the hope of enslaving us, the experience of mankind has too conclusively shown the splendid endurance of those who fight for home, liberty, and independence to permit any doubt of the result." In speeches before audiences of hard-pressed Confederate civilians in the fall of 1864, the president exhorted "a free and independent people" who were "fighting for existence" to continue the struggle, which would surely secure their liberty. In his script all the sacrifices, including conscription, imprisonment, privation, death, and destruction, would have a glorious outcome, independence and liberty. For Davis then, failure of the Confederate nation meant enslavement, the utter loss of rights and liberty, for Confederate citizens. Thus Davis probably would have difficulty accepting the separation Rable has devised.[11]

Based on my research, what is most striking in Confederate political history is the ineffectiveness of those politicians practicing Rable's "politics of liberty." I have found no broad opposition to Davis or to a Confederate government strengthened to wage war. In fact, I think many historians, Rable excluded, have been misled by the shrillness and extremism of opponents like Robert Barnwell Rhett in the viciously anti-Davis *Charleston (South Carolina) Mercury,* Representative Henry S. Foote of Tennessee, and especially the Georgians, Governor Brown, former cabinet member and army general Robert Toombs, and Vice President Alexander H. Stephens. From this group I exclude a man often included, Governor Zebulon B. Vance of North Carolina, because he does not belong. Davis correctly considered Vance a loyal Confederate who worked zealously for the cause, often with the president. Vance even managed to vanquish the major anti-Davis, anti-Confederate movement in his state.[12]

"Shrill" and "extreme" are nearly inadequate terms for describing the opposition leaders. Denouncing Davis as "vain, selfish, overbearing, ambitious, [and] intriguing," Foote shouted for "people to rise, sword in hand, to put down the domestic tyrant who thus sought to invade their rights." To Toombs the president was a "stupid, malignant wretch." One word sufficed for the vice president's opinion, "execrable." Alexander's brother Linton turned to a classical allusion, suggesting "perhaps" only a Brutus could save the Confederacy from the "little, conceited, dogged knave and fool."[13]

Yet for all their fulminations, those visceral opponents of Davis had practically no success. The Confederate Congress usually gave the president the legislation and the authority he requested. No matter the vituperation of Davis's political foes, Congress never acted in any significant way to curtail executive prerogatives. Even in Georgia, the home of the most luminous group of Davis enemies, Brown, the Stephens brothers, Toombs, and their allies could not carry the state into their camp. The president retained the support of both the state's senators, and the Georgia legislature never adopted a strong anti-Davis stance despite the opposition's efforts. Until the end of the war, no one doubted that Jefferson Davis was the president. In a real sense all the sound and fury was just that, sound and fury.

Returning to the two questions in the opening paragraph, my answer to both is negative. I do not detect any notable difference on the question of states' rights between the antebellum politician Jefferson Davis and the Confederate president. Before the war as well as during it, he professed a commitment to states' rights as he understood the term. That understanding entailed states' rights giving way to central power whenever national defense was the issue. As he made clear on so many occasions, Davis insisted that both the U.S. Constitution and the Confederate Constitution delegated to the respective central governments responsibility for national defense and the authority to carry out that responsibility.

Furthermore, I see little evidence that clamor over states' rights had much effect on the fortunes of the Confederacy or on the ultimate outcome of the war. Yes, opponents of Davis and his administration did at times utilize the vocabulary of states' rights, but they rarely did so with any effectiveness. There was almost an inverse relationship between the volume of the anti-Davis states' rights rhetoric and the accomplishments of those shrieking. Thus the influence and the importance of states' rights in the Confederacy, and especially in its demise, have been greatly exaggerated.

4

JEFFERSON DAVIS AND THE POLITICS
OF CONFEDERATE COMMAND

Before 1861, Jefferson Davis's chief occupation was politics. To be sure, he had other vocations. In early manhood he had served as an officer in the U.S. Army, and since the mid-1830s he had been a cotton planter. But from his selection in 1844 as a Democratic presidential elector in Mississippi, he had concentrated on politics, a dedication that resulted in a notable political career—holding seats at various times in the U.S. House of Representatives, the U.S. Senate, and the cabinet. In the 1850s Davis established himself as the dominant political figure in Mississippi. By the end of the decade, he had become a major leader in the Senate and in the nation, not just in his state and section.

Abiding by the conventions of his time, Davis claimed that he had no interest in appointive or elective office. Yet as his résumé shows, he had an overwhelming interest. He really did not want to remain on his Mississippi plantation but wanted to win office. To reach and then maintain his political position, he constantly campaigned and tended to constituent services. From 1845, when he entered the House, until the breakup of the Union, Davis was an absentee planter, spending considerably more time in Washington than in Mississippi. In 1860 he was a professional politician and an extraordinarily successful one. When the cataclysm of the secession crisis ripped the nation, it also tore Davis. He was no fire-eater, no sectional extremist. Although he believed in the constitutionality of secession, he never advocated leaving the Union. And he always identified himself as an American, one who looked to the flag "with the affection of early love." That his father had fought in the American Revolution gave Davis special pride. His own combat wound suffered during the Mexican War he counted as a badge of honor. Davis saw no contradiction between owning slaves as a representative of a slave state and devotion to his country. Rejecting the notion propounded by Republican politicians like Abraham Lincoln that the nation could not exist half-slave and half-free, he pointed to great American heroes like George Washington, Thomas Jefferson, Andrew Jackson, and Zachary Taylor, slaveowners all. Furthermore, the Constitution in his judgment protected slavery, a view shared by the U.S. Supreme Court.[1]

Even Lincoln's election in 1860 did not turn Davis into a secessionist. After all, fully 60 percent of American voters cast their ballots for candidates who had no problem with perpetuating slavery in the nation. In his state and to other southerners, Davis counseled caution. In the Senate, for himself and for his country, he strove to find a way to avoid the disintegration of the Union. He did not succeed. His own rhetoric trapped him just as the dynamics of southern and Republican politics trapped the country.

The failure of the Union massively affected Davis. The old politics, the style and system he had mastered, had failed. He believed that ambition and selfishness had led men to lose sight of the main goal, preserving the constitutional Union of the Founding Fathers. Davis called his departure from the Senate "the saddest day of my life" and never forgot 1861, when the Union he treasured disappeared. After the Civil War he would even sign the books he acquired on page sixty-one.[2]

For Davis, the creation of the Confederate States of America in February 1861 opened a new political world. It could not, would not, fail. The birth of the southern nation caught him in motion. He was throwing off the old politics but unsure of the new; he would have to find a new political center. Chosen president, Davis discovered that new core in his total commitment to the fledgling nation. "Our cause is just and holy," he announced to the Confederate Congress in April 1861. Over the next four years, words like "just," "holy," "noble," "sacred," and "sacrifice" filled his public statements and pervaded his personal letters.[3]

As president of the infant nation, Jefferson Davis would lead its quest for independence. For him that quest quickly became a crusade. He would make an indelible imprint on the political world of the Confederacy. That world included the military, for the Confederate Constitution, like its U.S. counterpart, designated the president as commander in chief of all armed forces. The military quickly assumed a central place because almost from birth the Confederacy found itself immersed in the cauldron of war. Only two months separated the establishment of the Confederacy and the firing on Fort Sumter. Of course, the military world would never exist in a vacuum divorced from the civilian universe. In the South, as in the Union, powerful bonds connected the soldiers and the civilians. In this essay, however, I will concentrate on the military, but even with that concentration my comments will reveal the inseparability.

In the South military affairs and operations were conducted in a political environment. This fact is fundamental. Too often those who discuss Confederate military history treat it as beyond or apart from politics, except for the individual politics of personality squabbles. That approach is absolutely wrong. The entire subject of Confederate military history is in a basic sense political. Of course, all American wars occur within a political framework. Yet a strong case exists to place the Civil War, for both sides, as the foremost political war.

This reality did not escape Davis. His antebellum background prepared him for it. He understood that political considerations formed the keystone of Confederate military policy. To a wartime aide he spoke of having "to conduct a war and a political campaign as a joint operation." His speaking of being compelled clearly indicates that combining the military and political did not please him; yet in his own words he never forgot "the necessity of consulting public opinion instead of being guided simply by military principles."[4]

It is impossible here to discuss all aspects of Confederate command and the politics of command. To make this study manageable, I will focus on Davis's actions and decisions in three critical areas, each central to the politics of command: strategic fundamentals, high-level appointments, and command relationships.

At the onset of the conflict, Confederates considered the size of their country, stretching more than a thousand miles from the Atlantic Ocean westward across the Mississippi to Texas, a strategic military asset. The Union faced an immense task to subdue a widely scattered population and occupy so much territory. But at the same time, this presumed positive posed a severe problem for the Confederate president. He would have defend the immensity, or at least make choices about which portions to defend, should the United States mount offensive operations sufficiently powerful to threaten the entire border.

When the Union did make precisely such an assault, the Confederate defense line was stretched far too thin, breaking at several points. Since the 1860s, critics have pounded Davis for failing to honor the great military principle of concentration. He should have decided, they argue, what areas were key and concentrated southern forces at these points.[5]

Such criticisms assume that the president as commander in chief dealt with military problems as hermetically sealed from all other influences. Davis knew better, however. He understood that decisions about what and where to defend in his far-flung country were political as well as military. Discussing that specific topic, in 1863 he informed his commander in the vast Trans-Mississippi theater that "the general truth, that power increased by the concentration of an army, is, under our peculiar circumstances, subject to modification." He went on to amplify, "The evacuation of any portion of territory involves not only the loss of supplies, but in every instance has been attended by a greater or less loss of troops." As a result each situation presented "a complex problem to solve." After the war Davis addressed his critics on strategic concentration. "It was easy to say other places were less important," he noted, "and it was the frequent plea, but if it had been heeded as advised, dissatisfaction, distress, desertions of soldiers, [and] opposition of State Govts. would have soon changed 'apathy' into *collapse*."[6]

Time and again political and military authorities both told Davis that loyalty depended upon defense. For many in Confederate uniforms, the great motive to fight came from defense of home against an invader. Home meant locality, maybe even one's state, but often did not extend beyond those boundaries. In 1862 this was especially true in Davis's far west, the Trans-Mississippi, where the commanding general reported citizens and state troops "luke warm" and "disheartened." The president fully comprehended that situation, assuring political leaders that "no effect should be spared to promote the defense of the Trans-Missi. Dept." To overcome any thought of local primacy, he asserted in July 1863 to the governor of Arkansas, "the states of the Confederacy can have but one fortune." Davis realized both that the war itself was forging a Confederate nationalism nonexistent before 1861 and that the process was as yet incomplete.[7]

For Davis, the supreme Confederate loyalist, the existence of this tentative allegiance was difficult to acknowledge. But accept it he did. He remarked on "the absence of any national character in our confederation." Confederate loyalty had to be built. Furthermore, he recognized the crucible of war as an extraordinary moment for its construction.[8]

Throughout the war Davis strove to meld the political and military. Of course, he did not always succeed, a fact that he recognized. Yet even the virtuoso Abraham Lincoln might not have succeeded completely. Still, Davis merits substantial credit for comprehending the fundamental political reality that he had to face in his strategic decisions.

In making major military appointments, Davis, as did Lincoln, had to contend with the civilian-professional quandary. Whereof leadership? No doubt can exist about Davis's preference. As a proud alumnus of West Point and a former regular-army officer, Davis had defended both the military academy and the regular army as an antebellum politician. As president of the Confederacy, he preferred professionals, and at the highest rank he placed only professionals. Every full general was a graduate of West Point and had seen service in the regular army. Yet Davis did not confuse his country with Prussia. He knew he would have to appoint political generals too. Practically speaking, there just were not enough professionals to staff the Confederate army.

In his appointments and assignments of officers, Davis took politics into account in two different ways. First, he wanted his political generals to have a positive effect on his administration and his cause. Second, even when dealing with professionals, he took seriously the view of political leaders in making assignments. Three illustrations make this point clearly.

Discussing appointments with Governor Isham Harris of Tennessee in the summer of 1861, Davis made clear his awareness of the political value accruing from the right choices. Harris expressed concern that the president had paid too little attention to previous political affiliations in awarding army commissions to Tennesseans. According to the governor, "positive political necessity" required more military slots for former Whigs. Explaining his initial selections, Davis responded, "the magnitude and supreme importance of the present crisis" had caused him "to forget the past." Yet he thanked Harris for advice that "shall not be disregarded" and urged him to write frequently and candidly.[9]

Likewise, in the summer of 1862, Davis faced a nagging political problem in South Carolina caused by the unpopularity of the general he had placed in command along the South Atlantic coast. At the center of this situation was John C. Pemberton, a Philadelphia-born West Pointer who followed his Virginia wife into the Confederacy. Pemberton was one of those officers who, without ever having done anything to warrant it, enjoyed an excellent military reputation, an opinion shared by Davis. The president considered him a selfless patriot committed to the Confederate cause. In the spring of 1862, Major General Pemberton, with headquarters in Charleston, assumed his duties as commander.

Despite his reputation, the transplanted Pennsylvanian never became acceptable to South Carolinians, especially Governor Francis W. Pickens, who urged Davis to remove Pemberton. Pickens said simply that the general could not generate public support, no matter his military standing. Although Davis defended Pemberton, amazingly calling him "one of the best Generals in our service," he realized that political considerations required a change. Having reached this conclusion, the president made a shrewd political-military move. When he reassigned Pemberton, he replaced him in September 1862 with General Pierre G. T. Beauregard, the victor of Fort Sumter and a favorite in South Carolina. Earlier that summer Davis had decided that Beauregard, the first Confederate military hero, was no longer fit to head a major field army, but the South Atlantic slot was an acceptable assignment because it entailed chiefly coastal defense requiring the engineering skills Beauregard possessed. Thus Davis found what he considered an appropriate position for a senior general and at the same time reaped the political profit from a grateful and pleased state governor and citizenry.[10]

The following year Davis counseled his Trans-Mississippi commander, Lieutenant General Edmund Kirby Smith, on the need to cultivate state officials. He knew that Smith could never meet all local demands, but he advised his general, "much discontent may be avoided by giving such explanations to the Governors of the States as will prevent them from misconstruing your action." Davis concluded that the governors could become Smith's "valuable coadjutors." Heeding this advice, Smith invited notables from the four states in his department to meet in Marshall, Texas. Governors, members of Congress, and other prominent men from Arkansas, Louisiana, Missouri, and Texas attended. The conferees, in published proceedings, proclaimed the fidelity of the Trans-Mississippi and their personal confidence in the cause. In this instance civil-military relations meshed perfectly.[11]

To this point in the war, Davis merits high marks for perceptiveness and attention to the political dimensions of his job as commander in chief. Although not always happy, he did not betray his prewar political professionalism. But in all politics, personal relationships are critical; they often determine success or failure. No political leader can maintain effectiveness if that person cannot deal effectively with people. By most accounts Davis too often failed in this regard. But why did he fail? Historians have employed an impressive array of pejorative adjectives and phrases to describe Davis's personal deficiencies: small-mindedness, self-righteousness, perverted loyalty, intolerance of dissent, cold. The list is legion.

But such exclamations provide little help in comprehending Davis's different interactions with different people. Instead, I think Davis's reaction to the disruption of the Union holds the basic clue. The failure of the old Union delivered a severe emotional and psychological blow to him. The new Confederacy must not fail, and to it he gave his absolute commitment. The old must be put aside; as he told Governor Harris, the crisis had caused him "to forget the past." To him the Confederacy had become "the noblest cause in which man can be engaged." No room remained for the human foibles that had brought down the once-glorious Union. Such notions as ambition, greed, vanity, and selfishness had to be banished from this sacred crusade. The Confederates, with Davis as their president, were embarked on a holy mission that had no place for the human comedy.[12]

In his own mind Davis was utterly selfless. "The cause" he told a Raleigh, North Carolina, audience in January 1863, "is above all personal or political considerations, and the man who, at a time like this, cannot sink such considerations, is unworthy of power." Davis had no doubt that he had sunk those considerations, believing that he had suppressed pride and overcome pain. Of course, he was at the top as the president and commander in chief, enabling him to conflate and to rationalize—to conflate his views with correct ones and to rationalize his selflessness and dedication only to a larger good, never to personal outlook and prejudices.[13]

The best way to understand Davis's motivation is to observe his dealings with three of his key generals. Each instance in its own way was critical not only for his performance as commander in chief but also for his cause.

At the outset of the war, President Davis liked and respected Joseph E. Johnston. Even a cursory look at their early correspondence, when Johnston was in command at Harpers Ferry, reveals a cooperative, even friendly, spirit. Then late in the summer of 1861, Davis sent to Congress the seniority list for the five full generals. When lawmakers created this highest rank in the army, they stated that rank previously held in the U.S. Army should govern placement in the Confederate army. But much to his dismay, Johnston found himself ranked fourth, not first, as he assumed would be his placement. Johnston was insulted; he was the only Confederate officer to have held the permanent rank of brigadier general in the old army and had no doubt that he should have headed this list.

Davis gave various explanations for his ranking. He claimed to have prioritized according to West Point class and standing within a class—Samuel Cooper, 1815; Albert Sidney Johnston, 1826; Robert E. Lee and J. E. Johnston, 1829 (ranked second and thirteenth within that class respectively); and Beauregard, 1838. The president also said he placed A. S. Johnston and Lee ahead of J. E. Johnston because they had been line officers, while J. E. Johnston's generalship derived solely from his staff assignment as quartermaster general. In addition, he asserted that the law applied neither to Lee nor J. E. Johnston because both had entered Confederate service from the Virginia state forces, in which Lee held the higher rank. While each of these reasons may have had some validity, Davis was clearly rationalizing what he had done. The oldest at age sixty-three, Cooper would always work as the army's adjutant and inspector general in Richmond, where he would sign a multitude of orders and directives. Davis wanted no questions about Cooper's authority. He believed A. S. Johnston to be his best soldier, and since his own arrival in Richmond, Davis had become increasingly confident in the Virginian, with whom he worked closely. Thus J. E. Johnston was relegated to fourth place.

Infuriated, Johnston would take none of it quietly. Angry and hurt, he penned a lengthy, agitated letter to the president in which he announced, "I now and here claim, that notwithstanding these nominations by the President and their confirmation by the Congress, I still rightfully hold the rank of first general in the Armies or the Southern Confederacy." After writing it, he held the letter for days before he decided that it exactly expressed his feelings and sent it on. In the words of his most important biographer, the general had written "an ill-judged and foolish letter" that should never have been forwarded.[14]

Davis was taken aback. Johnston's language was surely inappropriate from a military subordinate to a superior, but even more importantly, the letter told the president that his general cared more about rank than cause. Davis shared with his cabinet his brief, sharp reply: "I have just received and read your letter of the 12th instant. Its language is, as you say unusual; its arguments and statements utterly one-sided, and its insinuations as unfounded as they are unbecoming." This was the official end of any discussion. Never again during the war did the two men correspond about this matter, though its memory embittered Johnston for the rest of his life. In his reaction Johnston had revealed the human flaws of pride and ambition, which Davis could not countenance, for the Confederate purpose was far too serious to permit indulgence in such luxuries.[15]

One could step aside for a moment and consider how Abraham Lincoln might have handled a similar missive from an unhappy general. His response could easily have included a bit of humor, promising a new, even higher rank upon the general's producing a victory. After all, Lincoln would conclude that he and the country cared far more about victory than rank. But Davis, never.

This episode forever poisoned the Davis-Johnston relationship. For quite different reasons, neither man ever again trusted the other. Davis still respected Johnston's military ability, giving him important commands, the Department of the West in the fall of 1862 and the Army of Tennessee in December 1863, though Johnston's reputation remains a mystery. Yet Davis looked on this general as vain and ambitious, more committed to self than to the cause. Johnston never tried to improve the situation. Not only did he distrust Davis, but he also began associating with anti-Davis politicians. Imbibing their anti-administration line only inflamed his distrust. To his wife he asserted that the president, hoping he would fail, only gave him commands in which no one could succeed, though he would always act to ensure his reputation.

At almost the same time Davis's relationship with J. E. Johnston began to sour, he also experienced the degeneration of his faith in another full general. Davis had never been as close to Beauregard as he had been to Johnston. But nothing foreshadowed serious difficulties. The president was pleased with Beauregard at Fort Sumter and so delighted with First Manassas that he promoted the officer to full general in the field. Davis quickly became disillusioned, however.

The first instance occurred in the fall of 1861 with Beauregard's official report on First Manassas. The general filled this account with puffery strongly implying that he alone made victory possible and would have marched on Washington but for Davis's remonstrance. Additionally, he pointedly noted that even before the battle, the president had quashed his offensive plan. Poorly disguised as a mere battle report, this promotional tract was sent to friendly politicians as well as to the War Department.[16]

To Davis this kind of self-advertisement was unacceptable. A disgusted commander in chief told his general that if they "did differ in opinion as to the measure and purpose of contemplated campaigns, such fact could have no appropriate place in the report of the battle." More than anything else, Davis found intolerable Beauregard's "attempt to exalt himself." Making his fundamental point, the president said that he "labor[ed] assiduously in my present position," and "my best hope has been, and is, that my co-laborers, purified and elevated by the sanctity of the cause they defend, would forget themselves in their zeal for the public welfare."[17]

Despite his displeasure, Davis stuck with Beauregard, sending him west in the winter of 1862 to assist A. S. Johnston. Following Johnston's death at Shiloh in April, Beauregard assumed command of the most important western army, soon known as the Army of Tennessee, and concentrated his forces at Corinth, a strategic railroad junction in northeastern Mississippi. He informed the War Department that he would hold that post "to the last extremity." But when a powerful Union force approached, he retreated fifty miles southward to Tupelo.[18]

There Beauregard's relationship with the president collapsed. Davis already worried that this general, who appeared to write a great deal more than he fought, had been given responsibility beyond his ability. Then in mid-June Beauregard, without requesting permission from the War Department and even without prior notification, placed himself on sick leave and departed for a salubrious resort, putting his deputy in charge of the army. The president was appalled. A chronically ill Davis simply could not accept this conduct. In the cabinet, talk was about absence without leave, about desertion of his command. Once more in Davis's view, Beauregard had placed his personal concerns ahead of duty and cause. The president's fragile trust was destroyed. If Beauregard believed his army could do without him, Davis would not argue. On June 20 he removed Beauregard from command.[19]

Beauregard was furious. Feeling that a presidential vendetta underlay his removal, he castigated Davis as "that living specimen of gall and hatred." From that moment the general was convinced that the president would never give him a fair chance or a decent assignment. The gulf between the two men steadily widened. In one sense Beauregard was right: Davis consigned him in the military wilderness of coastal protection until the final autumn of the war, when he was utterly desperate for a senior commander.[20]

In direct contrast to his perception of J. E. Johnston and Beauregard as men who could not or would not subordinate the personal to the cause, Davis viewed Braxton Bragg as a selfless, dedicated patriot. Yet no other Confederate general would cause more controversy than crusty, fussy Bragg. Certainly Davis has received much of his harshest criticism for standing by Bragg for so long. My chief concern here is not whether or when the president should have sacked Bragg, though I will comment, but rather the basis of this seemingly ill-placed loyalty.

It all began at Pensacola, Florida, Bragg's initial posting. When his command there was substantially diminished to fill the ranks of the main armies, Bragg did not complain but did his work of organizing and training. That commitment impressed Davis, who saw a general who valued the cause above his ambition. He also thought Bragg was direct and honest with him. To his brother the president wrote positively about Bragg, noting that the general was in "no degree a courtier." What Davis learned in late 1861 about units trained by Bragg at Pensacola only added to the commander in chief's high opinion. His confidence grew so that by early 1862 he believed Bragg one of his ablest generals. From Pensacola in the winter of 1862, Bragg went to serve under A. J. Johnston. Positive reports from friends and family members on Bragg's performance at Shiloh and in Mississippi reinforced Davis's initial judgment. He soon made Bragg a full general.[21]

This impression had a profound effect on Davis. At this time his opinion of Bragg as a loyal Confederate differed sharply with the reservations he had begun to hold with J. E. Johnston and Beauregard, both of whom had initially enjoyed higher rank and more favored assignments. Davis's conviction about Bragg as devoted to his duty and to the cause had far-reaching repercussions. He stuck with the general as commander of the Army of Tennessee far longer than he should have. His commitment to the man was a key reason for his not cleaning out the viper's nest that made up the high command of that army. In fact, arguably his most disastrous command decision during the war was retaining Bragg as commander in October 1863, even after a personal visit to the army revealed the venomous relations rampant among its general officers. What makes Davis's inaction even more baffling is that he knew a poisonous atmosphere persisted even after his visit. To an experienced officer he assigned to the army, Davis wrote, "I rely greatly upon you for the restoration of a proper feeling, and know that you will realize the comparative insignificance of personal considerations when weighed against the duty of imparting to the Army all the efficiency of which it is capable." In this instance Davis's absolute conviction that the Confederacy demanded commitment to cause over anything personal became a mantra. Just a month later Bragg and the Army of Tennessee suffered a crushing defeat at Missionary Ridge just outside Chattanooga, Tennessee. Afterward both general and president realized the inevitability of change. Bragg resigned as commanding officer of the Army of Tennessee, never to return.[22]

In handling these three generals, Davis did not match the skills he exhibited in handling strategic fundamentals and major appointments.

In those two areas he acted as an able and politically sensitive commander in chief. But consumed with leading a holy cause and convinced of his own superhuman commitment to the Confederacy, he could not deal effectively with a commitment from others that was less than total. And he defined the boundaries and depth of that commitment. What was the best use of these three generals as well as others is not the issue here. But Davis did not attempt to employ them most advantageously. In the case of Johnston and Beauregard, he did not act toward them in a manner to get the most from them despite their flaws. With Bragg, the president's loyalty to his ideal overrode his judgment. Focusing on the politics of command reveals Jefferson Davis's strengths and weaknesses as commander in chief. In a great irony his incredible commitment to the Confederacy undermined its chance for success.

Jefferson Davis's pre-war plantation from an 1866 sketch in *Harper's Weekly*.

Jefferson Davis was inaugurated as the first president of the Confederate States of America on the steps of the Alabama State Capitol on February 18, 1861.

War-time residence of Jefferson Davis in the Executive Mansion at 1201 East Clay Street, Richmond, Virginia, 1865. *Library of Congress*

Jefferson Davis's office on the second floor of the Executive Mansion. Photograph by Katherine Wetzel. *Courtesy of the Museum of the Confederacy, Richmond, Virginia.*

The Custom House in Richmond, Virginia, 1865. Davis's war-time office was on the second floor. *Library of Congress*

Image of the Jefferson Davis Monument shortly after it was dedicated in Richmond, Virginia, in 1907. *Courtesy of the Virginia Historical Society, Richmond, Virginia.*

5

JEFFERSON DAVIS AND THE POLITICAL
DIMENSIONS OF CONFEDERATE STRATEGY

Many students of the Civil War would roll their eyes at this title, calling it preposterous. To suggest that politics might have had anything to do with Jefferson Davis as a strategist counters the general view, which pictures the Confederate president as anti-political, or at the least apolitical. In contrast I maintain that politics was never very far from Davis's strategic decisions. Emphatically he was a political man.[1]

Davis's prewar career was steeped in politics. In 1844, at age thirty-six, he campaigned throughout Mississippi as a Democratic presidential elector. The next year he matched that performance in a successful run for Congress. Because Mississippi in 1845 still had a general-ticket election for Congress rather than specified districts, Davis had to traverse the entire state. Then upon his return from the Mexican War, the governor appointed him to an empty seat in the U.S. Senate, a position he won on his own in the next election. To aid his party he left the Senate in 1851 to run for governor, a race he lost. But a year and a half later he joined President Franklin Pierce's cabinet as secretary of war. In that post, political considerations demanded much of his attention. In 1857, when Pierce departed the White House for New Hampshire, Davis remained in Washington, once again representing his state in the Senate.

Such a record clearly indicates that Davis's ambitions did not stop at the border of Mississippi. Although he had attained a dominant position in the Democratic Party in Mississippi, in the 1850s he also traveled and spoke in the North. To underscore his political stature, *Harper's Weekly,* a national news publication, early in 1858 devoted its entire front page to him, with an illustration, a biographical sketch, and a commentary in which the writer presented Davis as precise and moderate, not an extremist.[2]

His rivals in Mississippi politics never doubted his prowess or his strength. Those men, including the politically astute Albert G. Brown and the military hero John A. Quitman, respected Davis's power, even when they did not approve of his cause or admire him personally. Successful politicians in that state had to work for their triumphs. No one should think that in antebellum Mississippi, rich planters in mansions sipping Madeira dominated politics. Jacksonian political practices ruled in a rough-and-tumble world in which hard campaigning and attentiveness to the adult-white-male electorate were essential for success. Davis recognized those truths early on and never forgot them in his rise to dominance.[3]

When the men who created the Confederate States of America began looking at candidates for provisional president, Jefferson Davis's name appeared on almost everyone's list. No other active political leader from the Deep South had a stronger set of credentials; no one else had been more successful over the previous decade and a half. In February 1861 in Montgomery there was not a lengthy battle over the choice for president. Without serious or substantial opposition, Davis received the nod.[4]

Thus when Davis assumed the presidency of the Confederacy, he had an impressive political résumé. Yet the political dimensions of his administration remain relatively unexplored. Many people think that Jefferson Davis and politics were strangers. Three major reasons explain this often deeply held conviction. First, his wife, Varina, in her *Memoir* declared that her husband was never a politician and did not want the presidency. Instead he really wanted command of the army. The former assertion was no more than wishful thinking. As for the latter, Davis would have been pleased with the top military post, but he clearly indicated that he would accept whatever job the delegates in Montgomery gave him.

Second, after the war Davis seemed unpolitical in the traditional sense. He refrained from public comment on most contemporary political questions. His own *Rise and Fall of the Confederate Government* dwelt on the past, avoiding current affairs. In one sense, of course, it was quite political in its vindication of the South. But Davis did not present himself as a politician.

The third and final cause combines Confederate defeat and the imposing figure of Abraham Lincoln. Few individuals get tossed into the dustbin of American history faster than failed politicians, especially if they lose a war. And Davis surely failed, for the Confederacy suffered a massive defeat. Also, he is matched up against Lincoln, arguably the greatest of all U.S. presidents and certainly the ablest war leader. This comparison has been most cogently made by the superb historian David M. Potter. After cataloging Davis's abundant faults compared to Lincoln's superior skills, he suggested that a role reversal might even have resulted in a different outcome to the war. Potter has had numerous followers in his assessment of Davis's political ineptitude, though not all have made his direct comparison.[5]

But politics was never absent from the Confederacy. After all, the Confederate States of America resulted from a political act in which the leaders and citizens of seven Deep South states decided to sever their ties with the Union and create a new republic. Although not always agreeing with every decision along the road that led to the Confederacy, Davis surely participated in critical deliberations, and he made the entire journey. Moreover, he knew that the delegates in Montgomery who selected him as provisional president had made a political choice.

From the very beginning in the new nation, the political and the military were fundamentally inseparable. Davis understood this basic truth. He always believed that the political creation of the Confederate States would end in an arduous war with the United States. This conviction became reality when, only two months after his inauguration, hostilities erupted at Fort Sumter.

The crisis there graphically illustrates the intersection between military and political. Fort Sumter also required President Davis to make his first major command decision, one in which he had to weigh political repercussions. The presence of Union troops in the fort at the mouth of Charleston Harbor was but a minor military menace either to South Carolina or the Confederacy. They could not attack the mainland; besides the fort was under orders not to fire upon any vessels unless attacked. That had been the status of things since the fort's occupation by Union forces in late December 1860.

At the same time, Fort Sumter under Union control posed a major political threat to Confederate claims of independence. From the southern perspective, uninvited soldiers of another country occupied a fortification within Confederate borders. One of Davis's first acts as president was to send a diplomatic mission to Washington to negotiate for the removal of the Union garrison and the turnover of the fort to the Confederacy. Davis even was prepared to pay for the property. This is not the place to discuss the story of the Confederate delegation and the Lincoln administration except to say that no formal negotiations ever occurred. Moreover, during the first week in April, Lincoln had decided he would not peacefully relinquish Fort Sumter.

In Montgomery Davis and his advisers watched and waited. The diplomats in Washington stayed in touch with their government, reporting on conversations with officials and speculating about Lincoln's policy. Then on April 8 Davis learned that the governor of South Carolina had received a dispatch from Lincoln stating that a resupply expedition was being sent to Fort Sumter. Lincoln further stipulated that if not resisted, he would make no attempt at reinforcement with additional troops or guns "without further notice, or in case of attack upon the fort." This strategy would leave the calculus of power in Charleston Harbor apparently unchanged. It was a masterstroke, providing the first clear sign of the political genius that would make Lincoln such a formidable war leader.[6]

Now Davis had to make his first desperate decision. As he and his advisers viewed the situation, they occupied peaceful and defensive ground because the United States had no legitimate claim to Fort Sumter. Davis surely wanted peace; he did not want to use force. But with news of the resupply expedition, he recognized that "the idea of evacuation had been abandoned." In his mind any attempt to relieve or maintain the fort, whatever the term employed, was an assault on the Confederacy. Then the Union presence touched upon more than pride; it powerfully threatened the vital interests of his country. To a visitor he was blunt, "they meant to compel us into a political servitude we disown and spurn."[7]

Jefferson Davis made the decision to attack Fort Sumter. Although he had ultimate responsibility and never shirked it, he did not have to force his will upon his counselors. Potent arguments supported the case for action. The first, of course, was that Union occupation mocked the independence of the Confederacy. According to this outlook, the Confederate States of America could not stand as an independent nation so long as another power maintained an unwanted military force within its borders. Then officials in Montgomery worried with justification that despite Confederate military control in Charleston, hot-headed South Carolinians might on their own initiative assault the fort. Belligerent talk had circulated among zealots in and around Charleston for months. Such an action would undermine the authority of the Confederate government and commit it to a cause it had not decided upon. Finally the Confederate leadership realized that a move against Fort Sumter would galvanize the citizens behind their government and, even more important, probably propel the Upper South slave states, especially Virginia, into the Confederate fold.

The weight of these considerations pushed Davis toward action. There was but a single counterweight. Although contemporary evidence is scanty, Secretary of State Robert Toombs apparently argued against acting, asserting that in so doing the Confederates would lose all potential friends in the North. Toombs had no allies. All others in the deliberations concurred with the president that resupply could not be allowed. Although Davis recognized the difficulties that could stem from actually shooting first, he believed doing so essential. He told one of his generals, "There would be to us an advantage in so placing [the enemy] that an attack by them would be a necessity, but when we are ready to relieve our territory and jurisdiction in the presence of a foreign garrison that advantage is over-balanced by other considerations." Thus the first military engagement Davis ordered was grounded firmly in political reflection.[8]

Fort Sumter was not an isolated event. From his decision in Montgomery on April 10, 1861, onward, Jefferson Davis always acknowledged and acted upon demands of politics in making critical strategic decisions. Three examples, or case studies, from the war underscore the validity of this generalization—one at the outset and two from the midpoint.

At the beginning of the war, Davis decided he had to defend the entire frontier of the Confederacy along its border with the United States, from the Potomac River in the east all the way to Arkansas and Texas in the West, stretching more than one thousand miles. Without doubt, military and political considerations informed this decision. From the first Davis proclaimed the Confederacy only wanted to be let alone; it had no offensive ambitions regarding the Union. Thus he adopted a generally defensive posture. And following the beginning of hostilities, military necessity reinforced his initial defensive stance. Davis knew he lacked the means to send his forces northward, even though he told friends he wanted to make the enemy know firsthand the sting of war.

Yet as the conflict progressed, political concerns dominated Davis's strategic thinking. Comprehending the infant nationalism struggling to grow his country, he feared the fracturing of the Confederacy if the southern soldiers disappeared from any portion of it. He was convinced that any posture other than defending the entire Confederacy would undermine the new nation before its journey really got underway. The manuscript record underscores this pressure on President Davis. Even in late 1863, writing to one of his commanders, he emphasized the indispensability of overall defense: "the general truth that power is increased by the concentration of an army is under our peculiar circumstances subject to modification. The evacuation of any portion of territory involves not only the loss of supplies but in eve[ry] instance has been attended by a greater or less loss of troops, & a General, therefore, has in each case a complex problem to solve."[9]

Any valid appraisal of Davis's performance must take seriously the fact that he led a new nation, not an ongoing polity. In certain ways his task was more comparable to George Washington's than Abraham Lincoln's. In 1861 no traditional loyalty existed to the Confederate States of America. And nothing guaranteed maintaining the immediate loyalty that sprang up in the winter and spring of 1861. Between December 1860 and February 1861, seven states seceded from the Union and formed the Confederacy, their goal—protection from the perceived threat from the Republican Party taking control of the national government. After hostilities commenced at Fort Sumter in April, four more states joined the young country. If this new nation could not or did not provide protection, then any state might ask why remain in. This concern influenced Davis's decisions throughout the war.[10]

The second example is a crucial event from the middle of the war, the defense, or attempted defense, of Vicksburg, the citadel on the Mississippi River that protected and defended communications between portions of the Confederacy east and west of the great river. First, key figures besides Davis require identification: General Joseph E. Johnston, commanding the Department of the West; Lieutenant General John C. Pemberton, commanding at Vicksburg and a subordinate of Johnston; and Lieutenant General Theophilus Holmes and Lieutenant General Edmund Kirby Smith, each commanding the Trans-Mississippi Department, the former until March 1863 when replaced by the latter.

In the fall of 1862, Davis acted to bring stability and control to the vast area between the Appalachians and the Mississippi by creating the Department of the West. To lead this new command he appointed Joseph E. Johnston. The two key components in this arrangement were the Army of Tennessee and the Department of Mississippi and

Southeast Louisiana, which included Vicksburg. Davis really devised a theater command, which would become popular in World War II. When assigned to the Department of the West, Johnston was informed both orally and in writing that he had command authority over all forces, including general officers, in his department.

Despite that assurance and its repetition by the president and the War Department, Johnston found his post most uncomfortable. He claimed that he could not command without troops directly under his control. Rather than striving to become an effective commander, Johnston sulked, believing that Davis had put him in an impossible position, a title with no authority. But the authority was clearly there, an authority Johnston would never accept. Throughout his tenure in the Department of the West, Johnston kept up a mind-numbing correspondence with the War Department about his supposed powerlessness. No matter how many times reassurance about his real power came from Richmond, Johnston never stopped asking about it and never accepted his responsibility as a commanding general.[11]

The critical question facing these men in the spring of 1863 was how to deal with Major General Ulysses S. Grant's campaign against Vicksburg. Critical became acute when in April Grant passed below Vicksburg on the west bank of the Mississippi and then crossed to the east bank. Back in late 1862 Johnston advocated a concentration of Confederate forces to the area east of the river. Specifically he wanted at least a substantial portion of Holmes's force transferred to him from the west. When in Mississippi with Davis in December, Johnston pressed his case. The president agreed in large part, but he refused either to put Holmes under Johnston or to direct Holmes to do as Johnston desired.

Davis did, however, make his views clear in a letter to Holmes, a letter that he showed to Johnston. He told Holmes that defending Vicksburg was essential and went on to talk about the military value of concentration. Yet he issued no directive. Instead Davis told the general that he, Holmes, must use his discretion. Holmes would decide if the proper course would have his soldiers cross the river. Later, almost on the eve of Vicksburg's fall, Davis's instructions to Smith about the dire situation still left the new commander free to react as he thought best. No relief for Vicksburg ever came from the Trans-Mississippi.[12]

If Davis believed Vicksburg indispensable, and he basically concurred with Johnston on concentration, the question arises, why did he leave the decision to Holmes and later Smith? It was certainly not because of any reluctance to take troops from elsewhere to aid Vicksburg. The president had sent 5,000 men from the South Atlantic Coast, considerably farther from Vicksburg than Arkansas. It was surely not from a lack of interest. Even a cursory look at Davis's correspondence between December 1862 and July 1863 points to his commitment to Vicksburg, by the spring of 1863 even to his preoccupation with the city. In addition to the usual communications from civil and military authorities, letters from his brother Joseph underscored that the safety of his own home and family was also at stake. Even the president's reluctance to give specific instruction to his generals in the field did not dominate his thinking in this instance.

Davis made a political judgment. From the latter half of 1862 forward, he heard regularly from civilian and military officials about the situation in the Trans-Mississippi. Arkansas politicians continually pressed him not to denude the state of troops, forecasting dire results if that happened. They wanted concrete evidence that the government in Richmond was determined to defend their region. Nothing demonstrated that determination like troops on the ground. Responding to his commander in chief's letter, Holmes chorused that opinion. He said that if a substantial part his force went to assist Vicksburg, he probably could not defend the state. Even more, he feared that some soldiers would refuse to go east. After Smith assumed command, he did not alter Holmes's course. The force of the argument made by regional political leaders and corroborated by his generals made a deep impression on Davis. Several months after the fall of Vicksburg, he spelled out to Smith his thinking that the particular situation of the Confederacy demanded the defense of all its territory to retain allegiance to the Confederate nation. In sum, Davis's political judgment dictated his policy toward not using Trans-Mississippi troops for Vicksburg.[13]

Even while preoccupied with the defense of Vicksburg, Davis had to make another crucial strategic decision at this point in the war. Following his great victory at Chancellorsville in May 1863, General Robert E. Lee wanted to strike across the Potomac River, taking the war into enemy country. Davis listened carefully, for he knew full well that Lee was his best soldier; no other Confederate general had even approached his record against Union opponents. With his brilliant leadership, Lee and his Army of Northern Virginia had seized the initiative in the eastern theater. He also knew the preference of the president, who told his general, "I readily perceive the disadvantage of standing still."[14]

Yet some highly placed Confederates in Congress and in the military proposed a different role for Lee and his army. They urged a sharper focus on the West, promoting a "western concentration." Although a detailed plan never emerged, the intent was clear. Lee would go on the defensive and dispatch a corps from his army to the West. Once there it would join with Johnston and General Braxton Bragg to overwhelm the Federal army in Tennessee. Then the victorious, concentrated Confederates would relieve Vicksburg.

Having to decide between different views, Davis wanted to meet with Lee. In mid-May the general came to Richmond and presented a bold plan. He would take his army, with all the reinforcements the president would give him, and march into the North. To make his advance even more menacing to the enemy, Lee advocated stripping the Atlantic Coast and consolidating those troops under General P. G. T. Beauregard in central Virginia. From there Beauregard could pose a threat to Washington, tying down Federal troops. Moreover, he could quickly exploit any success the Army of Northern Virginia might win.

Lee had several goals for his offensive. He wanted to feed and supply his army on northern soil. Additionally, an invasion would carry the war to the enemy. He also believed his army almost invincible, certainly capable of inflicting a devastating defeat on any opponent. The prospect of a massive victory dominated his outlook; such a triumph could even lead to peace. It would surely relieve the pressure on the lower Mississippi Valley, particularly Vicksburg.

Before reaching his final verdict, Davis brought before his cabinet the question of whether to give Lee the permission or to hold him on the defensive, moving units of his army to the west. All supported Lee's thrust except Postmaster General John Reagan from Texas, who was so bothered that he asked Davis to reconsider. Aware of the gravity of the decision, the president agreed. According to Reagan, the cabinet spent an entire Saturday going over every issue in detail. An impromptu gathering on Sunday did the same. These meetings reaffirmed the initial decision, though. During these deliberations, Davis's thoughtfulness impressed Reagan: "His whole course of conduct showed him to be reasonable, conservative and just."[15]

Davis's deciding to go with Lee was understandable and sensible. His resolve had nothing to do with favoritism for the East. But it surely did have to do with Robert E. Lee, a proven performer. In contrast no one in the West, certainly neither Johnston nor Bragg, seemed to be rising to the occasion. Davis could not even get Johnston to exercise the power given to him. He certainly could not be certain what use would be made of troops sent from Lee. Would they arrive in time; more importantly, would they be effectively employed? Lee put it elliptically, writing of "the uncertainty of [their] application." Neither Davis nor Lee ever wrote overtly about their doubt, but both knew that decisiveness and boldness did not characterize Joseph Johnston's generalship.[16]

Without question Davis thought the political potential much better with Lee's advance. While the president authorized Lee's move, he did not strip the Atlantic Coast. To him that was too much of a gamble, for it risked losing Charleston and Savannah, possibly even the Carolinas. Those political dangers were too great. Still, Davis's goal was that Lee could provide what both men desired—a resounding triumph on northern soil. And his best general told the commander in chief he could deliver. Davis later wrote that he hoped Lee could win a battlefield victory in the North that would have "ensured peace on the only basis we were willing to accept it, independence." There certainly was a military dimension to Davis's election to back Lee; there almost always is in war. But in this instance the political motive was powerful, even dominant.[17]

I have not been arguing here that Davis always made the right choice among the alternatives he faced. I have not even maintained that he always weighed accurately the conflicting military-political risks in these crucial judgments. Nor have I suggested that he was a shrewd politician. But I do insist that he was a politician, a political man, who never lost sight of the political facets of any military design. Recognizing that about him is essential to understanding fully his strategic decisions.

6

JEFFERSON DAVIS AND THE WAR IN THE WEST

Jefferson Davis and the war in the West is such a huge topic that treating it thoroughly in a brief essay is impossible. But rather than resort to a sketchy overview of the vast and important subject, it is more valuable to examine two critical questions, both of which have occupied historians and indeed captured the attention of everyone interested the war.

First, did Davis comprehend the significance of the western theater, or instead did his living in Richmond, Virginia, lead him to relegate the West to secondary importance? Second, did Davis do a good job of managing the western war, or put more directly, did he succeed in the West as commander in chief? For the purposes of this study, the West covers the area basically from the Appalachian Mountains to the Mississippi River. The Trans-Mississippi theater will not be discussed herein except as it relates directly to events east of the river.

Of the two questions, the first is the easier. Just as many historians have claimed that too many of their number have focused too sharply on the eastern theater, likewise many have asserted that Davis did the same. Their argument goes something like this. Davis lived in Richmond, the Confederate capital, only one hundred miles from Washington. From there he riveted his attention on Robert E. Lee and the great contest for the two capitals. I disagree strongly with that opinion. There is no doubt that Davis not only understood the importance of his West but also deemed it utterly crucial. The evidence is simply overwhelming. Three examples make this point clear. The initial one predates 1861; the other two come from the war years.[1]

People often fail to remember that Davis did not move to Richmond until the late spring of 1861. He was from Mississippi, and for the quarter century before the war, home was a plantation in Warren County fronting the Mississippi River. In his experience the Mississippi was not just another river. Davis often went to Washington via steamboat on the Mississippi and up the Ohio. Moreover, he shipped his cotton downriver to New Orleans and traveled on the river to that metropolis for business and pleasure. Even before becoming a planter, his active-duty service in the U.S. Army centered on the Mississippi River Valley.

Thus when he became president of the Confederacy, Davis knew full well the importance of the great river. In September 1861 he created Department Number Two, the Confederate West, stretching from the Appalachians to the Mississippi and even beyond it. He placed in charge of this vast domain the man he considered the premier soldier in his army, General Albert Sidney Johnston. This is not the place to debate Davis's judgment about Johnston, but clearly he had an absolute conviction about the general's great ability.

Early in September, confined by illness to the second floor of the Executive Mansion, Davis recollected that he heard a familiar footstep, recognizing it immediately as Sidney Johnston's. He sent for the general to come up to see him. Although Davis knew that Johnston was en route to Richmond from the West Coast, he had not known when he would arrive. A brevet brigadier general in the U.S. Army, Johnston had been on duty in California as commanding general of the Department of the Pacific when he learned that his adopted state of Texas had seceded. Thereupon, he resigned his commission and started east.

Davis was delighted to have Johnston in Richmond ready for duty. "I felt strengthened and reassured," he wrote, "knowing that a great support had thereby been added to the Confederate cause." He had no doubt about the proper post for Johnston—the great West. In the president's opinion that command posed the greatest challenge in the new nation. And he declared Johnston the "only man who seemed equal to it."[2]

Of course, Sidney Johnston had a short-lived career in the Confederate army. He was mortally wounded at Shiloh on April 6, 1862, while rallying his troops on the front lines. Johnston's death hit Davis hard. He not only lost a friend but also a man he later termed "the great pillar of the Southern Confederacy." With Johnston, Davis concluded, "the best hopes of the Southwest lay buried."[3]

Whether or not Davis had placed Johnston on too high a pedestal, he never again trusted one man with so vast a command until R. E. Lee became general in chief in 1865. Yet in the West he tried to create what in World War II would become known as theater commands. On two occasions he organized most of the area between the Appalachian Mountains and the Mississippi as a single theater in order to bring more cohesion and control to an enormous geographical area: the Department of the West, under Joseph E. Johnston from the fall of 1862 to the summer of 1863; and the Military Division of the West, under Pierre G. T. Beauregard in the fall of 1864. Although both efforts failed, those outcomes and the reasons for them are not the issue here—it is Davis's attention to the West and his sense of its importance. And without question he understood its importance and in my judgment devoted to it the proper attention.

As I have argued elsewhere, including in this volume, Davis fully grasped the political dimension of the war. He knew full well that his West was more than boundaries on a military map. He realized that he had to rally the citizens of the region to the cause, just as he had to direct the military effort. On three different occasions—the winter of 1862–63 (December 9–January 4), the fall of 1863 (October 6–November 9), and the fall of 1864 (October 20–November 6)—he journeyed west to meet not only with armies and generals but also with civilian leaders and the general public. The first two trips took him all the way to Mississippi, but because of Union advances, the final one terminated in Alabama. In these forays into the heartland of his country, Davis made a number of major addresses and countless impromptu short speeches. According to the testimony of those who heard him and talked with him, the president's endeavors had a positive influence. Davis's Union counterpart, Abraham Lincoln, never did anything remotely comparable.

The evidence makes indisputable the verdict that Davis comprehended the centrality of his West and that he acted accordingly.

Now to the question of Davis's effectiveness, which is not the same as recognition and attentiveness because these do not automatically result in effectiveness. In this matter Davis's record is more mixed and my ultimate conclusion not so positive. In this essay I am going to concentrate on the year, roughly speaking, between the invasion of Kentucky in the fall of 1862 and the Battle of Chickamauga in September 1863. These months surely make up a critical period, arguably the time when the Confederacy had its greatest chance for success in the West. Four key events occurred during this crucial stretch of the war.

In September and October 1862, the Confederates launched an invasion of Kentucky. The Army of Tennessee, commanded by General Braxton Bragg, led the advance. In an underrated accomplishment, during the summer Bragg had transferred his army from northern Mississippi to Chattanooga, which became his jumping-off point for the invasion. Major General Edmund Kirby Smith, commander of the Department of East Tennessee with headquarters at Knoxville, joined the northward thrust. Between the two generals no question could come up about rank—Bragg was a full general, Smith but a major general. Yet for this operation Jefferson Davis as commander in chief never officially placed Bragg in charge of both forces. Instead, perceiving both officers as patriots in his own image, the president wrote Bragg that he knew "upon your cordial cooperation I can, therefore, confidently rely." A third key figure in what would transpire in Kentucky was the self-important Major General Leonidas Polk, Bragg's senior corps commander. Here I am not going to treat fully the campaign, which has several first-rate studies. My goal, instead, is to assess Davis's effectiveness as commander in chief.[4]

This drive to clear Tennessee of Union forces and to establish Confederate power in Kentucky started beautifully but ended dismally. Bragg and Smith moved smartly on parallel advances roughly one hundred miles apart into Kentucky. But once in the state, the Confederate drive quickly deteriorated. Bragg never attempted to command Smith; instead he asked Smith to join him in order to confront the main Union army. Smith refused, asserting that his own effort too important. The cooperation Davis expected as a matter of course never materialized. Furthermore, even in Bragg's own army disarray stalked; Polk failed to heed his commanding general's orders. The southerners, in a futile gesture, managed to inaugurate a Confederate governor of Kentucky and fight a bitter, bloody tactical draw at Perryville. Yet they did not succeed. After the stalemate at Perryville, the Confederates retreated. As Bragg and Smith fell back into Tennessee, Davis saw his high expectations thwarted. The entire venture was a strategic failure.

Recriminations filled the aftermath of defeat. Each of the three key generals complained to Davis, holding the others responsible for the outcome. Smith said he was not at fault, that Bragg's ineptness had lost the campaign and that he never wanted to serve under Bragg again. Polk boasted that had he been in command, the offensive would have been a glorious success. He tried to get other generals to call for Bragg's removal and went so far as to say that the commanding general had lost his mind. Shirking responsibility, Bragg announced himself blameless for anything that had gone wrong.

Realizing that no army could function amid these swirling accusations, Davis summoned the three generals to Richmond for individual conferences. He listened to each man state his case, and his response can only be defined as astonishing. He retained each in place, even promoting Polk and Smith to lieutenant general. The president lectured all that they must cooperate for the cause. The malignancy tearing at the vitals of the principal western army Davis left in place.

Not surprisingly, the problem plaguing the general officers of the

Army of Tennessee did not disappear. From Richmond, Davis watched and worried. Although he had not acted after Kentucky, he knew that the army could not succeed with pervasive dissension and turmoil. Moving to rectify the situation, he decided on a new command structure. In November he created the Department of the West, with General Joseph E. Johnston, returning to active duty following a serious wound, in command and having authority over both Bragg and the Army of Tennessee. Davis hoped to have in Johnston a steadying hand that would stabilize the agitation stirring the army.

The president left no doubt about Johnston's authority. Both he and the secretary of war made clear to the general that he had a command position, that every officer in the Department of the West, including Braxton Bragg, was his subordinate. Johnston's written orders were equally direct and explicit.

Still, Davis decided a personal visit to the army would help guarantee the harmony he so wanted. Thus in early December he left Richmond for a western tour that would take him as far as Vicksburg, though it began with a visit to the Army of Tennessee, encamped at Murfreesboro, Tennessee, between Nashville and Chattanooga. Accompanied by Johnston, the president spent the better part of three days with the army, reviewing troops, addressing soldiers, and speaking with officers. He thought the men in good shape and able to halt any Union advance.

But trouble had not gone away. On the last day of 1862 and the first day of 1863, Bragg and his army fought the bloody Battle of Murfreesboro (also known as Stones River). Although it ended in a tactical draw, Bragg realized that he could not maintain his army at Murfreesboro and retreated about twenty-five miles. Almost immediately the old rancor surfaced. A widespread judgment in the army called for the commanding general's resignation. A concerned Davis ordered Johnston to proceed to the army and report on whether or not Bragg should be removed. In his directive Davis reminded the department commander of his authority. Amazingly Johnston reported that all was well with the Army of Tennessee; he even praised Bragg. In reaching these conclusions he did not conduct extensive interviews, though he did talk to Bragg and a few other officers. During his inspection, Johnston had acted more like a guest than a commander.

Finally Davis ordered Johnston to assume command of the army and send Bragg to Richmond. In response Johnston said that Bragg's wife was ill, making it impossible for the general to leave, though he did not say what that had to do with his taking command. Johnston's major biographer argues that the general's sense of honor would not permit his relieving Bragg so that he could then assume command, considering this unseemly. Perhaps that was the case, but Johnston never showed any desire to assume responsibility as department commander. He spent most of his time wrestling with Richmond about his authority, which he never admitted to or acted upon. Faced with Johnston's interminable queries and refusal to act, the president seemed helpless and powerless. He did not relieve Johnston, who remained disgruntled and impotent; he did not relieve Bragg, who remained divisive and unpopular. Despite Davis's good and sound intentions in creating the Department of the West, it was not working. Since Kentucky nothing had changed in the Army of Tennessee.[5]

Events soon forced change, however. After March 1863 the focus shifted from Bragg and Tennessee to Lieutenant General John C. Pemberton and Mississippi. A West Point graduate and native Pennsylvanian who went with his Virginia wife into the Confederacy, Pemberton was one of those untried officers who had somehow accumulated an excellent military reputation, a view Davis shared. (After all, he placed Pemberton in charge of Davis's home territory.) Pemberton's actual command was the Department of Mississippi and Southeast Louisiana, which included the great river bastion of Vicksburg. Initially the general was well received by leading citizens of Mississippi. Of course, his department was a part of Joseph Johnston's command.

But what Johnston really wanted was control of the Trans-Mississippi, the huge area west of the river, and its troops. He believed this essential for the defense of Vicksburg and told Davis so. Johnston pressed his views on the president when both men visited Pemberton in Vicksburg in late December 1862. Davis would not extend Johnston's authority across the river, however, placing political considerations foremost. Rather than conferring upon Johnston what he wanted, Davis maintained the separate Trans-Mississippi Department. He informed its commander, Lieutenant General Theophilus Holmes, of Johnston's wishes and also noted the importance of combining forces, but he left the decision of sending troops east of the river to Holmes's discretion. But the general did not think he could safely dispatch men from Arkansas and sent no assistance. With justification, Davis feared that Arkansas might abandon the Confederacy if he pressed the issue. But even if he had acceded to Johnston's wishes for authority west of the Mississippi, one wonders what Johnston would have done with increased authority and responsibility. Regardless, the general was surely aware of both the importance of Vicksburg and Davis's worry about it.

When the Union threat to the Confederate stronghold accelerated with Major General Ulysses S. Grant's April 1863 crossing to the east side of the Mississippi below Vicksburg, Davis did not wait for Johnston to decide what to do. He promptly ordered him to repair to Mississippi. Someone was needed to control the situation, for Pemberton was outclassed by Grant. Upon arriving in Jackson on May 13, Johnston informed the War Department that because Union forces had inserted themselves between Vicksburg and Jackson, he had arrived too late. In his opinion, all was lost. Once again Johnston and Richmond became bogged down in a stupefying dialogue about his command authority. Although Johnston said only a quick strike could save Pemberton and Vicksburg, he orchestrated none. Davis urged action, wiring, "we cannot hope for numerical equality and time will probably increase the disparity." Meanwhile, the general was quarreling with the War Department on the precise number of men he actually had.[6]

Johnston's chief concern was to protect himself. Having concluded that Davis had placed him in a position where he could only fail, he wanted the record to show that he had been given an impossible assignment. To his wife's expressed concern about a blemish on his reputation, Johnston responded, "Don't be uneasy on the subject." Revealing some self-awareness, he told her, "I cannot be a great man, Nature and the President will it otherwise." He was half-right. Johnston possessed neither the moral strength nor the self-confidence for greatness as a captain, but the president wanted nothing so much as for him to prevail.[7]

Davis communicated daily with Johnston and Pemberton, but to no avail. All was lost. Vicksburg fell, and Pemberton surrendered his army of 31,000 men to Grant. Davis agonized over the disaster, craving to know whether the calamity had resulted from "mismanagement, or it may have been that [victory] was unattainable." He was convinced that he had done all he possibly could to give his commanders on the scene the means to defeat Grant. Pemberton he viewed as a brave soldier leading brave soldiers. The troops did exhibit heroism, and their commander was undoubtedly brave, but bravery alone never won a battle. Davis never perceived the reality that Pemberton was overmatched by Grant.[8]

Exempting himself and Pemberton left only Johnston as the villain. Without doubt the departmental commander bore much responsibility. He had done practically nothing with what he had, even after admitting he faced a grave crisis. Caution and self-protectiveness were his watchwords. Davis wanted a court of inquiry, which he believed would indict Johnston's performance. One was called, but it never convened. For the beleaguered Confederates, the pressure of war would not permit such luxuries. But Davis was solely responsible for the command structure and the commanders who did not function effectively. Given the personalities involved, success was most unlikely.

Ten weeks after the surrender of Vicksburg, the Army of Tennessee won the greatest Confederate victory in the West at the Battle of Chickamauga, just south of Chattanooga. This triumph should have been the occasion for a great celebration, even if the defeated Union army did manage to withdraw into Chattanooga. But that rejoicing did not occur, not with the toxic atmosphere enveloping the senior general officers in the army. In fact, just as the fighting began and even while it intensified, backbiting and sniping reverberated through the battling army. At the forefront of this poisonous band were Bragg and Polk, this fully a year after the Kentucky campaign.

My goal here is not to establish fault, though there is plenty to go around, enough to tarnish all, but rather to appraise Davis's reaction. Word of the recurrent trouble quickly reached Davis. An aide on a western fact-finding trip telegraphed from Atlanta that the situation called for the president's personal attention. Startling occurrences shook the army, though they should not have been surprising. Lieutenant General James Longstreet, who had come from Virginia to the Army of Tennessee and had fought at Chickamauga, wrote that Bragg should be replaced, as did Polk. Polk even told Davis that Bragg's weakness derived from "wickedness." For his part, Bragg relieved Polk of his corps command and pressed charges against him. Additionally, the other corps and division commanders initiated a petition, eventually signed by a dozen generals, demanding Bragg's relief.[9]

In October, only three weeks after Chickamauga, Davis arrived at the Army of Tennessee encampments just south of Chattanooga. This was his second trip in less than a year to this courageous but mishandled army. He rode through the camps and talked with soldiers, but his main task was dealing with the strife and disorder among the general officers. He held discussions with Bragg and his subordinates. Everyone had a chance for their say, which they frankly delivered. Davis confronted a major command decision.

Incredibly he left Bragg in command, though he did reassign Polk and allow Bragg to relieve another corps commander. Yet the president left in place the ravenous malignancy that had been devouring the army for more than a year. As commander in chief, this was arguably the worst and most damaging decision Davis made during the war. Even more baffling, he realized that he had temporarily bandaged a wound that required a drastic remedy. He admitted as much to an experienced lieutenant general he reassigned to the army: "I greatly rely upon you for the restoration of a proper feeling, and know that you will realize the comparative insignificance of personal considerations when weighed against the duty of imparting to the Army all the efficiency of which it is capable." To the hapless Bragg he employed what in this instance was no more than a mantra. Circumstances, Davis implored, "should lift men above all personal considerations and devote them wholly to their country's cause." The hard-fighting, loyal troops of the Army of Tennessee deserved much more from their commander in chief.[10]

To answer the two questions posed at the beginning of this essay, Jefferson Davis fully understood the importance of the Confederate West, and he devoted sufficient time and energy to it. Still, he was largely ineffective in managing the western war. While some of his decisions, such as assigning Albert Sidney Johnston and creating the Department of the West, have positive attributes, others, chiefly his dealing with interminable tumult among the generals in the Army of Tennessee, do not. Overall, what he did and even more what he did not do hampered the Confederate cause far more than it helped the war in the West.

7

JEFFERSON DAVIS AS WAR LEADER

As president of the Confederate States of America, Jefferson Davis led his country in its war against the United States. The Confederate Constitution followed the U.S. Constitution in giving the president the basic powers of commander in chief. Thus in wartime the Confederate president would lead the political and military effort. Davis certainly possessed the requisite qualifications to become commander in chief, a war leader. In fact few who have led this nation in war from the War of 1812 to Iraq could match his pedigree. He had military, political, and administrative experience that set him apart from other southern notables in 1861.

Davis's particular background was immensely influential in his selection as provisional president of the fledgling Confederacy. He had graduated from West Point, had spent seven years on active duty as an officer in the regular army, and had a distinguished combat record as a regimental commander during the Mexican War. Additionally, he had been a member of both the U.S. House and Senate, serving in the latter body during the 1850s as chairman of the Committee on Military Affairs. Furthermore, between 1853 and 1857 he held the office of secretary of war under President Franklin Pierce.

Despite these impressive credentials, Davis has usually been harshly judged by historians in his starring role, president of the Confederate States. This historical assessment almost makes a prima facie case for disregarding prior achievement and experience in awarding high and responsible office. Of course, Davis is usually matched against his wartime opposite, Abraham Lincoln, and invariably comes in second, generally a distant second. Yet trailing Lincoln does not automatically brand Davis a failure, for in my judgment Lincoln was clearly the greatest war leader in our history.

But even when viewed alone, Davis commonly receives poor marks. Without going into an extended historiographical discussion, it is safe to say that most historians have been and still are quite critical of the Confederate president. In general they portray him as brittle, ill-tempered, and unable or unwilling to grow with responsibility. According to this script, these shortcomings were especially disastrous in his inability to appreciate the political dimensions of the war he was fighting and in his micromanagement of his generals.[1]

Before assessing Davis as war leader, it is essential to begin with the criteria used to judge an individual's performance as war leader. While making no claim for including every possible category, most everyone would agree on the centrality of three: first, understanding the political and strategic reality facing the country at war; second, articulating war goals or aims in relevant and understandable terms and communicating them to the citizenry; and third, managing the war as the military commander in chief. Considering how Davis performed in each of these areas will provide a perspective for assessing him as a war leader.[2]

Jefferson Davis was convinced that an armed struggle between the South, striving for independence, and the North, resisting it, would be long and bitter. From his tenure as secretary of war and as a leader in the U.S. Senate, he understood the potential war-making power of the North, both human and material. The formation of the Confederate States of America did not alter his outlook. When hostilities began only two months after his inauguration as provisional president, he acted accordingly. Expecting a lengthy conflict in which the

Confederates "would have many a bitter experience," he called on Congress to accept enlistments for the duration, or at least three years. In contrast, congressmen, confident of a short, happy war, wanted only six months of service. Despite his urging, Davis could get but one year as a compromise.[3]

As the war progressed, he moved smartly to try to make his side more competitive. This is not the place for a detailed discussion of his actions, but two examples, one from early in the war, another from late, should make the point. In the spring of 1862, Davis proposed and obtained from Congress the first national conscription act in American history. Then in the final winter of the war, he moved against considerable opposition to sever the powerful southern bond that had bound black slavery to white liberty. Davis successfully advocated putting slaves in Confederate uniforms, realizing that such an act would mean emancipation, at least for slave soldiers, and fundamentally alter southern society. But he was willing to jettison slavery to save Confederate independence.

Davis also comprehended that material limitations sharply restricted his military options. Early on, many Confederates clamored for their troops to take the offensive, to take the war to the enemy and to enemy territory. Davis agreed in principle but recognized that he could not equip his armies for such an undertaking. He could see no good in announcing that the Confederacy had shifted to the offensive when he could not back up such words with actions. That situation he explained to his generals, though not to the Confederate public. Even in the face of criticism, he did not think he could explain his reasoning. "I have borne reproach in silence because to reply by an exact statement of the facts would have exposed our weakness to the enemy." Davis could only "pine for the day when our soil shall be free from invasion and our banners float over the fields of the Enemy." Reality governed.[4]

The president's fathoming the position of his country involved more than objectivity concerning military resources. From the outset Davis understood that he led a nation in the making, that Confederate nationalism was being constructed during the war. In the autumn of 1861, he urged brigading troops by state because he saw "state pride" as "the highest incentive for gallant and faithful service."[5]

Moreover, he perceived that the fragility of Confederate nationalism, even Confederate loyalty, must govern military strategy. Davis felt that he must temper the military maxim of concentration. The president believed that he had to maintain a visible military presence throughout the country or he would face "dissatisfaction, distress, desertion of soldiers, and opposition of State Govts." In 1863 he wrote one of his commanders: "the general truth, that power is increased by the concentration of an army, is, under our peculiar circumstances subject to modification. The evacuation of any portion of territory involves not only the loss of supplies, but in eve[ry] instance . . . troops." Davis could envision a reaction so vigorous that it could cause the disintegration of the Confederacy. He struggled constantly with the vexing problem of concentration.[6]

This tenuous nationalism did not shake Davis's conviction about the ultimate outcome, for he always looked to the American Revolution as the cauldron of American nationalism. Although admitting in a public address in January 1863 that war was utterly evil, the president defined "the severe crucible" as essential, for it alone could "cement us together." He believed that the horrors of war "we have been subjected to in common, and the glory which encircles our brow has made us a band of brothers, and I trust, we will be united forever." Now, he asserted, soldiers of every state had become "linked in the defense of a most sacred cause." To him the war was creating Confederate nationalism.[7]

For President Davis, his new country had a single major goal, independence. He viewed the Confederacy as engaged in a struggle matching that of the Founding Fathers—liberty versus despotism. In defining this contest he proclaimed in his inaugural address as provisional president that the Confederacy "illustrate[d] the American idea that governments rest upon the consent of the governed, and that it is the right of the people to alter or abolish governments whenever they become destructive of the ends for which they were established." He emphasized to his fellow Confederates that they were defending the rights they had inherited from their Revolutionary ancestors. Throughout the war he accentuated the intimate relationship between the patriots of the founding generation and the patriots endeavoring to create the southern nation.[8]

As a seasoned professional politician before 1861, Davis was aware that public support was necessary for the success of public policy as well as for the success of a public official. His emphasis on liberty and the sacred link between two generations of founders certainly resonated with his constituency. Southerners had been evangels for liberty and the holiness of the Revolution since the Founding Fathers. Davis pointed to the roster of southern heroes from George Washington forward who had defended liberty. Now under the Confederate banner, their sons and daughters were emulating their example.

In this clarion call to defend liberty, Davis did not dodge slavery. He knew the peculiar institution was at the center of southern society, of the Confederate States. Even so, he insisted that he was not directing a war for slaveowners but for white liberty. White southerners understood perfectly, for at least since the Revolution they had considered their liberty inextricably tied to black slavery. To them, only southern whites could make decisions about slavery; any outsider interfering with the institution threatened white liberty.

In this context Davis stood on traditional southern ground when he condemned Lincoln's Emancipation Proclamation. He interpreted this edict as a manifestation of the brutal war being waged against the Confederacy. He asserted that his government had thwarted all efforts by an aggressive United States. Unable to vanquish "a people determined to be free," the Union, according to Davis, had turned to barbarity, even including the possibility of massacre in the countryside and a horrendous race war, which to the minds of white southerners would be the inevitable result of any general slave uprising. In Davis's judgment the alternatives faced by the Confederates were stark: victory and liberty or defeat and enslavement.[9]

Although Davis clung to liberty as the Confederate goal, he responded to a changing war. By 1863 the course of the struggle had brought real hardship to much of the home front. In his holy quest for liberty, Davis led the Confederacy in directions inconceivable in 1861. He told southerners that they must fight for liberty, no matter the cost. From conscription to enlisting slave soldiers, Davis asked for the previously unthinkable. But he was no dictator. He led but also heard and heeded both leaders and private citizens in an effort to ensure that government policy did not stray too far from public opinion. For example, the president listened to the outcries against the substitution provision of the conscription law, which permitted a drafted man to escape service by paying for a substitute; to critics it allowed the rich to avoid serving and arrayed class against class. In 1863 Congress, with Davis's support, repealed substitution and even made those who had purchased substitutes eligible for service. The United States had a similar substitution provision, but it remained in place for the entire war. As a veteran of antebellum Mississippi politics, Davis well knew the political danger of even seeming to favor the rich. He envisioned no rich man's war with poor men doing the fighting. Tax policy also shifted. Congress enacted a progressive income tax and placed a 10 percent tax in kind on agricultural products, with the proceeds to be distributed among soldiers' families.

In addition, the president hailed efforts by states and localities to assist those deprived by war. The Confederacy did fall short of fulfilling the needs for assistance, yet seven decades before the New Deal and under extremely difficult circumstances, it tried, however stumblingly. For Davis and his administration, significant relief could come only when battlefield success could relieve pressure on the home front.

From all the letters that crossed his desk, the president had no doubt about the profound sacrifices many Confederates were making. In his public statements, especially by 1864, he always praised their commitment and devotion to the cause, though he admitted he could not predict "how many sacrifices it may take" to achieve victory. Acknowledging in 1864 that many soldiers had absented themselves from the army, Davis never cast aspersions on their patriotism. He realized that these men had gone to war to protect liberty and defend home and family. Yet by late 1863, with home and family often undefended while confronting privation, social disorganization, and advancing Federal armies, many soldiers rethought their primary duty.[10]

Davis understood what was happening and was not impervious to the motivations. Examining the files of men sentenced to death for desertion made a powerful impression. In one case a soldier left his unit upon being informed that the enemy had driven his wife and children from their home; they were all sick and destitute, and one child had already died. This husband and father departed without permission, though he did return, whereupon a court-martial convicted him of desertion. Noting that he would have acted precisely as the soldier did, the president set aside the conviction and ordered the man restored to the ranks. Faced regularly with this hard reality, Davis urged those who had gone home to return to their units. Homes and families could ultimately be protected, he maintained, only by battlefield success. In his mind there was but a single alternative: "slavish submission to despotic usurpation."[11]

As president, Davis strove to get his message before the Confederate public. His formal messages to Congress along with proclamations appeared in newspapers, as did public addresses. Yet he went further. On three occasions—in the winter of 1862–63, in the fall of 1863, and in the fall of 1864—he traveled from the capital of Richmond across much of his country, on the first two occasions all the way to Mississippi, on the third to Alabama. These trips had a military purpose, for he visited with armies and their commanders. But he also met with civilian authorities and with the public. Davis made countless public appearances and delivered numerous speeches, from formal presentations before legislatures to impromptu remarks at railroad stops. He did not hide in Richmond but tried to make himself seen and heard by his fellow citizens.

On the whole he succeeded. Although a multitude of political adversaries slashed at him, especially from 1863 on, no single politician rose to challenge seriously his leadership. His shrill opponents howled, but they accomplished little. These men were strongest in Georgia, where inveterate antagonists Governor Joseph Brown and Vice President Alexander Stephens led the assault. Still, Georgia remained stalwart for the president. As late as 1864 Brown and Stephens failed to turn the state legislature against Davis. Until the bitter end he remained the dominant political force in the Confederacy.

While Davis never shunned his role as leader of the Confederate people and nation, he took quite seriously his position as commander in chief of the armed forces. The president considered himself an expert on military matters and believed himself eminently qualified to command an army or to command commanders. He never doubted his own military ability or judgment. In directing the Confederate war, Davis adopted hands-on tactics. His own predilection as well as his sense of duty involved him in all aspects of the military, from the trivial, such as complaints from junior officers, to the deadly serious, such as critical strategic decisions. His administrative style dated to his time as U.S. secretary of war. Then presiding over a small establishment, he wanted to know about everything and see every document. He brought that same practice to the Confederate presidency. Nothing changed, not even by 1862, when he was directing a great war. The minutiae that received his regular attention utterly boggles the mind. He questioned nominations for junior officers and involved himself in deciding whether two pieces of artillery went to the navy or to Charleston. A letter from a captain wanting a transfer from Virginia to the Mississippi Valley received presidential attention. The list is unending.

Davis was his own secretary of war. While he did have men, all but one quite able, in that office, he did not create areas of responsibility nor did he delegate authority. He wished for advice, often requesting it, and willingly discussed issues, large and small, but he made the decisions. Although directives that left Richmond carried various signatures, including at times that of the secretary of war, all contained decisions made by Jefferson Davis. Running the war office or the high command, Davis was definitely a micromanager.

Yet he did not deal with his generals in the field in the same manner. Although he appointed the general officers who commanded his armies, once he put them in place, he rarely told them what to do. His instructions in June 1861 to General Joseph E. Johnston at Harpers Ferry set the tone. Informing the general that he wanted Harpers Ferry held as long as possible, the president said that as commander on the scene, Johnston must exercise his own discretion. Likewise, three months later Davis acted similarly when, against the president's wishes, Major General Leonidas Polk violated Kentucky's neutrality by occupying Columbus. There was an immediate political backlash; an alarmed governor of Tennessee warned the president that Polk's move harmed the Confederate cause in Kentucky. Davis then countermanded Polk, but the general insisted that his actions were militarily indispensable. Responding, Davis asserted that "the necessity must justify the action," which meant Polk, the commander on the scene, would make the final decision. He stayed in Kentucky.[12]

Davis pursued that policy throughout the war, though he would recommend courses of action. In the spring of 1862, he suggested to General Albert Sidney Johnston that he isolate one element of the enemy and inflict a mighty blow. But the decision was Johnston's. Again, in the winter of 1862–63, he urged Lieutenant General Theophilus Holmes in Arkansas to assist Joseph Johnston in Mississippi but tempered his language by telling Holmes that he must use his own discretion. Additional examples could be brought forth. It is difficult to explain the contrast between Davis's handling of his field commanders and his management of the War Department. The difference was certainly not because he failed to comprehend the change wrought by the telegraph. Throughout the war he utilized that instrument, fully aware that it permitted rapid communication between him and his generals. Perhaps it came from his military background—generals should be left alone. Possibly his service in Mexico with General Zachary Taylor, whom he admired extravagantly, influenced him, for Taylor growled about interference from civilian authorities above him. Whatever the reasons, Davis gave his generals enormous leeway.[13]

Not only did Davis fail to direct his generals, but he too often left them in command long after they should have been removed. Unlike

Lincoln, Davis did not regularly relieve generals. Of course, one of the most famous incidents involving Davis and his generals was his firing of Joseph Johnston in 1864 before Atlanta. Yet that action did not occur because Johnston failed to obey orders from Richmond, but instead because he refused to tell Davis what he, Johnston, intended to do. Even so, this is the exception that proves the rule.

A much more common situation prevailed after the failed Confederate advance into Kentucky in the fall of 1862. Confederate misfortune in Kentucky came from several directions. At the same time, the inability of Confederate commanders to cooperate was surely crucial. Following the Confederate withdrawal, the three senior generals—two army commanders, Braxton Bragg and Edmund Kirby Smith, and Bragg's ranking subordinate, Leonidas Polk—all blamed each other for the outcome. Davis thought highly of each officer, considering all of them loyal, selfless patriots. He saw them as he had earlier described Smith to Bragg: "He has taken every position without the least tendency to question its advantage to himself, without complaint when his prospects for distinction were remote, and with alacrity when danger and hardships were to be met." Yet the failure in Kentucky terribly disappointed the president. As a result he brought the three men, individually, to Richmond, where he listened to each deflect responsibility and accuse the others. After hearing these recriminations, Davis, incredibly, left the three in place, even promoting Smith and Polk, and implored them for the good of the cause to get along. When fundamental overhaul was desperately needed, Davis stood still.[14]

And there were other examples of this kind of response or nonresponse. For the possibility of the ultimate Confederate success, they happened far too frequently. In such instances, for all the right reasons, a ruthless, even pragmatic, commander in chief would have instituted dramatic changes, including dismissals, transfers, and promotion of junior generals. In the Army of Tennessee, the cancer that Davis did not even attempt to excise in the post-Kentucky weeks was left to grow even more virulent.

Jefferson Davis as a war leader performed far more ably in his political role than in his military one. Concerning the political dimensions of his position, broadly construed, he merits high marks. On the military side the result is mixed. Davis did comprehend the strategic situation facing his country, and his basic strategic decisions were reasonable and understandable. But as a purely military commander in chief, he exhibited serious flaws. Too often he did not exercise appropriate command authority over generals or intervene effectively when crippling disagreements divided senior commanders. Elsewhere I have delineated the practical and emotional reasons behind his inaction. Simply put, Davis did not have the steel or ruthlessness to make absolutely essential command decisions.[15]

8

JEFFERSON DAVIS AND
THE MEANING OF THE WAR

In the dozen years before 1861, Jefferson Davis was a national politician who became increasingly influential; by the latter half of the 1850s no southern political leader had more standing or prestige in the nation. Then during the Civil War, his occupying the presidency of the Confederate States ensured his prominence. Throughout the many years he lived after the war, he occupied a formative and powerful role in creating the Lost Cause ideology, which included establishing both the causes of the war and the war aims of the Confederacy.

During the antebellum years, when Davis served as a U.S. senator from Mississippi on two separate occasions (1847–51 and 1857–61) and as a member of President Franklin Pierce's cabinet (1853–57), the question of slavery in the territories became the major national public issue. It initially focused on the effort to outlaw slavery in the Mexican Cession, the vast area added to the United States as result of the Mexican War that included the Southwest and California. Congress struggled unsuccessfully for an answer until in 1850 the Compromise of 1850 seemingly solved the problem. But that solution was short lived. In 1854 the passage of the Kansas-Nebraska Act, which repealed the Missouri Compromise line dividing slave and free territory in the Louisiana Purchase, set off another political conflagration. Despite a U.S. Supreme Court decision in 1857 that supposedly rendered a final judicial verdict, slavery in the territories remained both dominant and flammable until the Union divided. Throughout these years of public debate, legislation, and court opinion, Jefferson Davis was vigorously active.[1]

Of course, differing outlooks on slavery in the territories derived from opposing views of slavery in the nation. On this central institution in southern society, Davis never flinched. He called slavery a "paternal institution" sanctioned by "the decree of God." As he explained to a friend, "it is time for our justification before the uninformed and that we may be understood by posterity as well as by contemporaries that the long continued and gross misinterpretations of our slave institutions should be answered." To Davis slavery was not a necessary evil but a positive good that permitted the great mission of civilizing and Christianizing an inferior race and that simultaneously underlay white equality. Publicly and pointedly he stood foursquare behind the institution that he had known since childhood and provided the foundation for not only his family's prosperity but also that of his state.[2]

On the political matter of the territories, Davis was equally forthright and adamant. Following the basic reasoning laid out by John C. Calhoun, the foremost political champion of slavery and the South, Davis maintained that the Constitution protected slavery as property. Therefore, southerners as Americans had every constitutional right to take their slave property into the national domain. "Shall the citizen, who rejoicing in the extended domain of his country, migrate to its newly acquired territory," he asked Congress, "find himself shorn of the property he held under the Constitution?" His answer was a resounding negative. Considering veterans of the Mexican War like himself, he posed the question: "Shall the widow and orphan of him who died in his country's quarrel be excluded from the acquisition obtained in part by his blood?" As he saw it, there could be only one response: "Never, Never! Reason and justice, constitutional right and national pride, combine to forbid the supposition." Davis felt vindicated when the Dred Scott decision essentially adopted Calhoun's interpretation, declaring that Congress could not prohibit slavery in the territories.[3]

He accepted Calhoun's assertion that the territorial question placed at stake "the equality of the South." In Davis's judgment anti-southern northerners raised the issue for "political strife, for sectional supremacy." Unlike Calhoun, Davis never recognized a substantive moral dimension in the antislavery movement and territorial prohibition initiatives. He defined antislavery and anti-South activity solely as striving for "a discrimination against one section of the [country], the palpable object of which is totally to destroy political equality." Confronting this assault, Davis proclaimed that the South must resist, for his section could never "consent to be a marked caste, doomed, in the progress of national growth, to be dwarfed into helplessness and political dependence." Such a state of affairs would mean that the South had lost its precious legacy of liberty.[4]

Looking carefully at Davis's reaction to the vexing and volcanic territorial issue makes one point quite clear. He did not talk about states' rights; he did not see the restriction of slavery as violating that principle. Instead he emphasized that the exclusion of slavery from the territories would torpedo the constitutional rights of slaveowners and shatter the equality of the South in the nation. Thus his concern focused on individuals and section.

At the same time, states' rights did make up a central part of Davis's political vocabulary. Throughout his antebellum political career, Davis lined up behind the states' rights orthodoxy that claimed the allegiance of the Democratic Party and, for that matter, many other southerners outside that party's tent. He viewed Thomas Jefferson and James Madison, with their Virginia and Kentucky Resolutions of 1798 and 1799, as the architects of the political gospel. He also held in high regard the leading states' rights apostle of his day, Calhoun. Davis considered himself but a disciple of these giants of constitutional interpretation. In this reading of the Constitution, the states had created the federal government and in so doing delegated only specific powers to the central authority. Thus the federal government had only the limited powers spelled out in the Constitution. Carried to its logical conclusion, as Davis and most southerners did, this doctrine meant that the states that had separately and voluntarily joined the Union could also separately and voluntarily leave it. He gave voice to this conviction in his final speech in the Senate, averring "as an essential attribute of State sovereignty, the right of a State to secede from the Union."[5]

Even so, Davis's analysis of the political world of the late 1850s and the danger facing the South had little to do with states' rights. He defined the growing Republican Party as a distinct threat to his section and its central social and economic institution. He decried the self-proclaimed Republican mission of prohibiting slavery in the territories and attacking slavery as a blemish on the nation. As he saw it, the party's goals disregarded the constitutional rights of southerners as Americans and endangered the southern social system. In trying to defame southerners and challenge their "Americanness," Davis found Republicans reprehensible. In his mind their "greatest evil" had already occurred: "the perversion of the Northern mind and . . . the alienation of the Northern people from the fraternity due to the South." If these Republicans should gain national power, then he perceived palpable danger to the South and slavery.[6]

Again Davis concentrated on the Republican menace to section and slavery, not states' rights. In the crisis of the Union following the election of Abraham Lincoln in November 1860, Davis maintained that focus. He hoped for a compromise between the Republicans and the South that would protect southern rights as he defined them. He was no fire-eater preaching the glories and joys of secession. In his own state Davis tried to defuse the excitement over Lincoln's election, and in Congress he worked for a settlement. On both fronts he failed. Mississippi rushed toward secession, while Congress stalled, thwarting adjustment.

Finally and reluctantly, Davis concluded in late December that the Union would dissolve. To protect slavery and southern power, secession became mandatory. At that point states' rights moved to the forefront because that doctrine legitimized breaking up the Union. In his farewell address to the Senate, Davis pointed to states' rights as the constitutional bulwark upon which Mississippi and the other seceding states stood. Yet his remarks left no doubt that secession was warranted, not because the rights of Mississippi or any other state had been violated, but because slavery and the safety of the South had become endangered. The Republican Party had mounted "an attack upon [southern] social institutions" that necessitated secession.[7]

Mississippi joined with six other Deep South states to form the Confederate States of America, and Davis was chosen as provisional president. In his inaugural address in Montgomery, Alabama, in February 1861, he made clear his conviction that the new nation was the legitimate descendant of the American Revolution. He told his audience that the South had "asserted a right which the Declaration of Independence of 1776 had defined to be inalienable." Because the Union of the Founding Fathers "had been perverted from the purpose for which it was ordained and had ceased to answer the ends for which it was established," the states of the Confederacy acted peacefully to end the government created by compact and brought into being one of their own.[8]

Upon Davis's arrival in Montgomery and even before his inauguration, he underscored the foundation upon which the young nation rested: "Fellow Citizens and Brethren of the Confederate States of America—for now we are brethren, not in name, merely, but in fact—men of one of flesh, one bone, one purpose, and of identity of domestic institutions." Pointing to what he called the "homogeneity" in the Confederacy, he said it would surely prevail. He perceived unity in purpose and allegiance to a single goal, the success of the new nation. The Confederacy would guarantee the liberty of its citizens, a freedom that included the maintenance of slavery. For white southerners this conjunction of white liberty and black slavery came directly from the Revolution. From at least that period, whites in the South defined their liberty, in part, as their right to own slaves and to decide the fate of the institution without any outside interference.[9]

In striving to ensure their liberty, Davis and his fellow Confederates ended up in an increasingly brutal war. By the summer of 1862, Davis saw horror becoming pervasive in his countryside. The penetration by Federal forces into so many areas of the South brought thousands of civilians into direct contact with raids, battles, and occupations. Some Federals welcomed the havoc wreaked upon persons and property, while others for a time tried to control the destruction. But boundaries proved impossible to maintain. In a public proclamation Davis denounced an enemy who "laid waste our fields, polluted our altars, and violated the sanctity of our homes." In a message to Congress, he did not mince words: "Humanity shudders at the appalling atrocities which are being daily multiplied under the sanction of those who have obtained temporary power in the United States."[10]

For Davis, the Emancipation Proclamation represented the culmination of the savage war waged on his country. Abraham Lincoln issued his preliminary proclamation in late September 1862, with the final version promulgated on January 1, 1863, the date it took effect. Using his authority as commander in chief, Lincoln freed all of the slaves in states and areas of states still engaged in rebellion against the United States. Across the Confederacy the edict generated an outrage; Confederates saw it as inciting slaves to rebel, which threatened a ferocious bloodbath and the possibility of a race war. In a message to Congress, Davis condemned the proclamation as "the most execrable measure recorded in history of guilty man." To him the proclamation represented the "impotent rage" of a government that could not triumph by defeating Confederate armies.[11]

Davis wanted mightily to retaliate against what he saw as an increasingly cruel foe. That his armies had not yet reached into the territory of his opponents restricted his options, denying him the opportunity to impose civilian suffering and destruction that came only with invading hosts. His only realistic course was to turn on prisoners of war. But if the Confederates violated accepted practices and began executing prisoners, even in the name of retaliation, they would become just as savage as their enemy. Even more important, the Lincoln administration would surely do likewise to the prisoners held by the North. Despite his growing scorn for his opponents, Davis never did discover an appropriate way to repay what he viewed as barbaric ferocity.

Amid the conflagration engulfing his country, President Davis did not say much about states' rights. In his inaugural he had acknowledged "the sovereign States now composing the Confederacy," and periodically he stated his long-held belief in the doctrine. Although he never spent much time discussing states' rights, his political opponents used it as a club to pound him. Holding up such measures as conscription, impressment, and the suspension of habeas corpus, they attacked Davis for creating a consolidated central government. Despite the fact that Congress had legislated on all these measures, Davis's critics accused him of being a despot, running roughshod over the rights of states and citizens.[12]

Facing this criticism, Davis remained unperturbed. His position was clear, and he stated it forthrightly. The nation must defend itself. He insisted that the Confederate Constitution authorized Congress to raise an army and provide for defense, which legitimized the very steps his antagonists railed against. This *constitutional* view of defense or security did not originate with the war. Back when he was secretary of war in Pierce's administration, Davis advocated federal construction of a transcontinental railroad, arguing that protection of the West Coast and of citizens demanded that action. Opposition by his southern strict-constructionist friends did not sway him then; nor did the wartime fault-finders deter him.[13]

For Davis nothing could override the importance of bringing the war to a successful conclusion. To him that meant Confederate independence and the resulting liberty of the nation's citizens. In the end Confederate salvation even caused him to reconsider the sanctity of slavery. In the anguished winter of 1865, with disasters coming from every direction and catastrophe looming, he moved to break up liberty and slavery, the longstanding cement of southern society. He agreed that slaves should become Confederate soldiers and urged Congress to pass the appropriate legislation. He also fully comprehended that creditable military service would lead to emancipation, at least for those who served. Furthermore, as he vowed to the governor of Virginia, he was even prepared to give the slave veteran "a right to return to his old home when he shall have been honorably discharged from military service." Davis, therefore, committed himself to freedom plus the right of the ex-slave to live as a free man at his former home, the property of the individual who had previously owned him. To save his nation Davis found himself standing in a place utterly inconceivable in 1861. He was willing to challenge the privileges of private property and contemplate a quite different postbellum society: whites, slaves, and a substantial, albeit unknown, number of free blacks, who had been enslaved, all living on the land of the white propertyowner.[14]

The southern landscape after 1865 did differ sharply from the antebellum era, even more dramatically than Davis's new world would have altered it. The Confederacy was crushed by military force. Slavery disappeared; ruin and poverty marked the devastation wrought by the war. Davis himself spent the first two postwar years in prison and the remaining twenty-two years trying, unsuccessfully, to recreate prosperity for himself and his family. His various failed ventures are not the subject here, however.

Davis was in the forefront of those formulating the Lost Cause ideology. That role without question made up his most important postwar activity. He made his contribution in three different formats: private correspondence, public appearances and addresses in the 1880s, and the publication in 1881 of his *Rise and Fall of Confederate Government*. Throughout the letters, the speeches, and two fat volumes, two major themes dominated. First, Davis always insisted on the constitutionality of secession, which in his mind meant that the secessionists possessed the legal and moral right to sever the Union. Thus in opposing secession and especially in employing force against secessionists, the federal government was wrong. Second, in his interpretation the Confederacy was defined as engaging in a noble fight to uphold constitutional liberty, vindicate the rights of the states, and resist consolidation.[15]

Davis's absolute conviction that in 1861 he had acted in conformity with the Constitution underlay his refusal ever to ask for pardon or for the removal of political disabilities imposed on him by the Fourteenth Amendment. That men he admired, even revered, such as his older brother Joseph and Robert E. Lee requested and accepted pardons did not budge him. He readily agreed that he had taken an oath to uphold the Constitution, and he insisted that he had done so even in supporting secession. In 1876 Davis explained to a congressman, "further it may be proper to state that I have no claim to pardon not having in anywise repented or changed the conviction on which my political course was founded as well as before as during and since the war between the States." But there was more. To those who asserted that a petition for pardon or removal of the disqualification stipulated by the Fourteenth Amendment did not necessarily mean admission of wrong, Davis was equally adamant. "Now sir," he lectured a friend, "if I were to ask having my disabilities removed, it would not be a confession of wrong doing on my part, but it would be to that extent an admission of right to impose the disability I asked them to remove. That neither you nor I can concede." He clung to that creed as long as he had breath.[16]

Yet nowhere in Davis's exposition of Lost Cause ideology, either in its antecedents or content, did slavery appear. In this instance, as with focusing on the constitutionality of secession and the nobility of the Confederate cause, Davis joined with the other founders of the Lost Cause. Slavery disappeared from discussions of war causation and the Confederacy.[17]

Davis made his fullest statement on the role of slavery in *Rise and Fall*. These two labored, massive volumes do not constitute a memoir in the traditional sense but contain an extended apologia for Davis's interpretation of secession and the Confederacy. In his book he downplays slavery as causing secession. "The truth remains intact and incontrovertible," he wrote, "that the existence of African servitude was in no wise the cause of the conflict, but only an incident."[18]

That announcement contrasts fundamentally with Davis's clearly expressed view in 1861 and before that he regarded slavery as basic to secession and the Confederacy. But Davis and his fellows in the Lost Cause effort in the 1870s and especially the 1880s did their work stunningly well. Their gospel, that secession was about the Constitution and states' rights, not about slavery and sectional power, persuaded the South and, even more importantly, the nation. That interpretation of the coming of the war dominated nationally for a long time, into the second half of the twentieth century. Moreover, it remains amazingly vibrant even in the twenty-first century.

The historical record makes clear that Jefferson Davis's views did not remain the same. Between the antebellum years and the 1880s they changed. My understanding of the man is that he was sincere in both of the stances he took. How then should his position or positions be explained? Fastening on what he thought and said at the time, in the extended crisis over the fate of the Union, offers the most honest understanding. Then he concentrated on slavery and sectional power as the causes of secession, not violations of states' rights. Although states' rights provided constitutional sanction for secession, Davis and his fellow southerners in 1860 and 1861 left the Union to protect slavery and what they defined as southern liberty. They created the Confederate States to guarantee the preservation of both.

9

JEFFERSON DAVIS AND TWO MONTGOMERY INAUGURALS, 1861 AND 1886

The first inauguration of Jefferson Davis in Montgomery, Alabama, occurred in February 1861. That event is well known and its importance indisputable. The second, as I term it, took place twenty-five years later in April 1886. That occurrence is little known and its importance largely unrecognized. Yet the initial ceremony was essential for the one that followed a quarter century later, which overmatched in significance its predecessor.

Basic similarities linked the two inaugurals. In each instance Davis received an invitation to travel to Montgomery. Each time he made the trip by train. On both journeys an enthusiastic public cheered him as he made his way toward Montgomery. In the city, in 1886 as well as in 1861, a massive turnout and an adoring welcome awaited him. But he never stayed long in the Alabama capital, just over three months in 1861 and but a few days in 1886.

At the same time, sharp contrasts differentiated the two occasions. In 1861 Davis, a political figure of national importance, had been summoned to Montgomery to lead a new southern republic, the Confederate States of America, in its quest for independence. In 1886 Davis, an old man of seventy-eight and in poor health, had been invited as an honoree to attend a celebration—the dedication of a monument to

Confederate soldiers. This second time in Montgomery, Davis himself became a living monument. White citizens anointed him as the symbol of a revered, albeit selective, Confederate memory.

In 1861 Davis had resigned his seat in the U.S. Senate following Mississippi's secession and returned to his riverfront plantation just south of Vicksburg. On February 9 he received a telegram informing him that he had been chosen provisional president of the Confederate States of America and calling him to Montgomery. On the eleventh a slave rowed Davis out into the Mississippi River, where he boarded a steamboat for Vicksburg. When the vessel reached that river port, a gala throng, complete with bands and militia units, celebrated the president-elect. From there he took a train some fifty miles east to Jackson, the state capital, where more citizens praised the native son. To reach Montgomery from Jackson by rail, Davis had to go north to Grand Junction in Tennessee (a state still in the Union), then east to Chattanooga, south to Atlanta (within Confederate borders), and finally southwestward to Montgomery, the Alabama capital that served as the Confederate capital. "One continuous ovation," as a reporter put it, characterized the five-day journey. Along this route of applause, Davis spoke at almost every stop, except in Tennessee.[1]

The president-elect's train pulled into Montgomery at 10:00 P.M. on the sixteenth. A large, excited crowd and salvos of artillery noted its arrival. Davis spoke briefly to the gathered listeners, then headed for his hotel. But the clamor for more from the new chieftain did not subside. At 10:45 he appeared on the hotel balcony to emphasize his sense of the moment: "Fellow Citizens and Brethren of the Confederate States of America . . . we have henceforth, I trust, a prospect of living together in peace, with our institutions a subject of protection and not of defamation." He stressed what he called the "homogeneity" of Confederates. And he made clear the centrality of its slavery in the young country and its citizenry's commitment to the institution.

Davis's inauguration was set for Monday the eighteenth, which gave him Sunday to rest and work on his address. Inauguration day dawned cloudy and cold, with frost on the ground. At 10:00 A.M. a parade formed in front of his hotel, headed by a brass band and followed by militia companies in sky blue pants and bright red coats. Davis and Vice President Alexander H. Stephen of Georgia followed in a barouche lined with saffron and white, mounted with silver, and drawn by six magnificent gray horses. Carriages with other dignitaries and ordinary citizens along with people on foot completed the lineup. As the procession moved toward the Alabama statehouse, perched on a commanding hill, the sun broke through the overcast. Thousands of cheering spectators filled the streets and sidewalks. Some five thousand more waited on the capitol grounds.

There the official party took seats on a wooden platform erected on the front patio of the capitol. At 1:00 P.M., "amid a storm of applause," Davis rose and faced his huge audience. In his remarks the provisional president touched upon several themes, but he forcefully enunciated two. He connected the Confederates of 1861 with their forefathers of 1776. Asserting that the Declaration of Independence trumpeted the inalienable rights of the people to establish a government that would guarantee liberty and domestic tranquility, Davis pictured southerners as acting on that principle. For him the wondrous government established by the Founding Fathers had been subverted "by wanton aggression" and no longer served "the purpose for which it was ordained, and ceased to answer the ends for which it was established." Confederates, he declared, clung to their heritage. "The Constitution framed by our fathers is that of these Confederate States." In his interpretation their "exposition of it" provided "a light which reveals its true meaning."

At the same time he praised "a people united in heart, where one purpose of high resolve animates and actuates a whole." As he had in his comments on the night of his arrival in Montgomery, in his inaugural he proclaimed the "homogeneity" of Confederates would ensure the preservation of the new nation. Although he never used the word "slave" and never spoke overtly about this key institution in southern society, he left no doubt about his reference. For him and his listeners, simultaneous allegiance to the Founding Fathers' gift of liberty and to slavery posed no problem. They saw no contradiction, for in the South, from at least the Revolution forward, white liberty and black slavery were inextricably intertwined.

In the evening hundreds attended an inaugural reception. Davis spent much time shaking the hands of well wishers. Women as well as men showered him with accolades. But Davis well knew that he had not become a master of ceremonies for a festival. He recognized that he had taken on an immense job. He had to build a government from nothing. As he wrote to his wife, "We are without machinery without means and threatened by a powerful opposition but I do not despond and will not shrink from the task imposed on me." His tasks became virtually Herculean, for within two months a great war engulfed him and his country. And in another six weeks, he and his government moved to a new capital, Richmond, Virginia.[2]

Between that transfer to Richmond and Davis's return to Montgomery in 1886, his world and that of the South would be fundamentally transformed. Defeat in war resulted in impoverishment for the South and for Davis. Moreover, he spent the first two postwar years imprisoned at Fort Monroe, Virginia, facing a charge of treason. From his release in 1867 and for the rest of his life, he struggled to support himself and his family. Yet during all the years and tribulations, Davis never doubted either the virtue of the Confederate cause or the rightness of his own actions between 1861 and 1865. He detailed his version of secession and the war in his two-volume *The Rise and Fall of the Confederate Government,* published in 1881.

The year 1886 found Davis living at Beauvoir on the Mississippi Gulf Coast near Biloxi. He had come to this substantial seaside home in 1877 as a guest of its owner, Sarah Dorsey, who revered him. When she died two years later, she bequeathed Beauvoir to him. It was the former president's home until his death in 1889.[3]

In March 1886 the mayor of Montgomery went to Beauvoir to invite Davis to be an honored guest in the city in late April. This time the occasion was not openly political but rather the laying of the cornerstone to a monument for the Confederate dead from Alabama. The city officials extending the invitation assured him that they would make his journey as comfortable and easy as possible, coming for him and providing transportation. Davis agreed; in fact he decided to make a short tour by accepting requests that he also participate in ceremonies in Atlanta and Savannah afterward.

When the time arrived, the mayor of Montgomery and a delegation of dignitaries went by rail to escort their honored guest. They traveled in a private railroad car that would take them and Davis back to Montgomery. The trip turned out to be another great ovation. Whenever the train stopped, enthusiastic crowds gathered. Flowers and other gifts poured on him. A reporter claimed that "half a car-load of floral offerings" had been "showered" upon Davis.[4]

The train puffed into Montgomery around 8:00 P.M. on March 27. It was eerily like 1861—fireworks lit the sky, and the rebel yell reverberated through the evening air. Even a steady rain dampened neither turnout nor excitement. An eyewitness reported that the noise only increased as Davis approached his hotel, the Exchange, the same one he had stayed in a quarter century earlier; he was even given the same room, number 101. The aroused crowd chanted for a speech. An exhausted Davis was led out onto the veranda from which he had addressed an equally receptive audience back in 1861. But this time the old man could only utter a few words, "With a heart full of emotion I greet you again."[5]

The next morning the rain continued but stopped around noon. Then a barouche led by four gray horses followed by uniformed militia took Davis up the hill to the Alabama capitol, where the throng of thousands "broke into the wildest cheers, which were long and hearty." On the arm of the mayor, Davis walked up the steps. Just as he reached the spot where twenty-five years earlier he had taken the oath as provisional president of the Confederate States, rain began falling again. An old Davis friend in the audience, Virginia Clay-Clopton, recalled: "I saw women, shrouded in black fall at Mr. D's feet, to be uplifted and comforted by kind words. Old men and young men shook with emotion beyond the power of words on taking Mr. Davis's hand, and I feared the ordeal wd. Prove the death of the man."[6]

Davis spoke briefly, though the roar was so "long drawn out that it seemed for a time that he was not going to get a chance to speak." His words repeated what he had so often said. The virtue and justice of the Confederate cause formed the thrust of his observations. A united South, he told his listeners, rushed to defend principles when the "thunder of war came ringing over the land." And of the war he stated: "It was that war which Christianity alone approved—a holy war for defense."[7]

The ceremonial laying of the cornerstone took place on the twenty-ninth. For this event "the sun shone warm and bright." A parade identical to that of the previous day marched up to the capitol; just to the right of the building, the monument was to be erected. On this day Davis addressed his audience more formally. A reporter recorded that he "spoke with great earnestness and in tones easily heard by most of the large crowd present." Once more he chorused his familiar themes. A united South had nobly defended honored principles. As he put it, "one sentiment inspired all classes." At the forefront stood what Davis termed "State sovereignty." According to him, Alabama and other southern states acted to protect their constitutional rights, which had been violated by an aggressive North. Asserting that he did not want to discuss the old political issues, he insisted that he only "review [ed] the past . . . in vindication of the character and conduct of those to whom it is proposed to honor on this occasion." He considered sacred "the belief in the righteousness of our cause and the virtue of those who risked their lives to defend it." Nowhere in this speech, however, did Davis mention the "homogeneity" and "identity of domestic institutions" that he had used in 1861 to underscore the centrality of slavery in the new southern republic.

After the address, received with "long continued applause and cheers," Davis attended a reception in the governor's chambers in the capitol. After a midday meal at the Exchange, he joined his hosts in decorating the graves of Alabama's war dead. On the thirtieth he departed for Atlanta; he had been in Montgomery for two days and three nights.[8]

To the Alabamians along the rail line and in Montgomery, Davis was obviously a hero. On the night of his arrival in the city, "a great piece of fireworks extending nearly across the square [in front of the Exchange] was set off, making in flame the words, 'Welcome, Our Hero.'" This sentiment, so graphically expressed in Montgomery, pervaded the entire South. Davis was a living link to the past, a past white southerners wanted to cherish. The great war chieftains Stonewall Jackson and especially Robert E. Lee were long dead. Senior generals, like Pierre G. T. Beauregard and Joseph E. Johnston still lived, but neither enjoyed widespread adulation. Controversy surrounded both men, and besides, neither had known notable battlefield success after the first few months of the war. Moreover, Davis's imprisonment meant to most white southerners that he had suffered for them. If he merited prison, all did, for they did not think that they had done anything wrong. White southerners designated him "their representative man," who had been "true and faithful to the trust which had been reposed in him."[9]

Of these two ceremonies occurring in Montgomery a quarter century apart, the first, Davis's inauguration in 1861 as provisional president of the Confederacy, is far better known than the second, his role in 1886 dedicating a monument to Confederate war dead. In addition, conventional wisdom holds that the former has considerably more historical importance than the latter. Here, I enter a challenge to that view. While certainly not trying to minimize the significance of the Confederacy and the Civil War in the country's history, the 1886 event had a powerful emotional and political influence on how Americans thereafter viewed the war and its meaning.

The pageant in Montgomery heralded the preservation of Confederate memory in a particular fashion—a memory defined by former Confederates, from Jefferson Davis on down. This distinct memory has become known as the Lost Cause ideology. Its central theme depicts a virtuous southern white people nobly defending their liberty against the threat of tyranny, initially in following the Founding Fathers to create a separate republic, then on the battlefield against a brutal, invading host. This portrayal totally omitted one subject, however. It never mentioned slavery as having any part in the southern decision to secede and break up the Union or in the formation of the Confederate States.[10]

This script included no chorus to Davis's declaration in his farewell address to the Senate back in 1861 that Mississippi and other southern states had to react to the belligerent and unconstitutional assaults on slavery by aggressively antislavery northerners. Davis underscored that motive in a message three months later to the Confederate Congress in April 1861, declaring that a monomaniacal antislavery Republican Party threatened the South's central institutions. Facing such a mortal threat to "interests of such overwhelming magnitude," Davis concluded, the people of the South had to act "to avert the danger with which they were openly menaced." In the secession crisis, from the Atlantic seaboard to Texas, southerners constantly echoed Davis's cry: fanatical Republicans intended to doom the South by destroying slavery. In the words of one Georgian, to avoid "the extinction of slavery," his state had "to dissolve her connexion with the General Government."[11]

With slavery banished, the Lost Cause interpretation of secession and the Confederacy became increasingly visible across the South. In the late 1880s and 1890s, organizations like the United Confederate Veterans and the United Daughters of the Confederacy preached this gospel and guarded it against heresy. Monuments remembering the gallant Confederate warriors, just like the one Davis helped dedicate in Montgomery, soon dotted the region. The most imposing were in Richmond, the former capital of the Confederacy and in consequential ways the capital of its memory. Arrayed along Monument Avenue are four heroic statues of the Confederate pantheon.

While it conquered the South, the Lost Cause had an even more massive effect. Carried beyond southern borders by evangelizing believers, their explanation of secession and the Confederacy gained widespread acceptance throughout the nation. This Lost Cause had impressively greater staying power than the historical Confederate States; the latter lasted but four years, while the former dominated national consciousness until well into the second half of the twentieth century. Even in the twenty-first century, it is amazingly alive and well. Thus Jefferson Davis's second inaugural in Montgomery should be recognized for its far-reaching influence.

ACKNOWLEDGMENTS

Transferring my remarks prepared for oral presentation to the printed page, I was always mindful of the assistance given by my initial audiences. Comments and questions from those who heard me speak have certainly prompted me to clarify my language and tighten my arguments. I am indeed grateful to the institutions that provided the occasions for me to discuss Jefferson Davis. They are: Kentucky Historical Society, Library of Congress, Pamplin Historical Park, Southeastern Louisiana University, University of Alabama, University of Mississippi, University of Richmond, University of Virginia, and Vicksburg National Military Park.

In addition, I am grateful to another institution and to several individuals. My own Louisiana State University over the years has generously supported my research and scholarship. Dr. Lynda L. Crist, editor of *The Papers of Jefferson Davis,* has been a steadfast supporter since I began working on Davis. She even kindly agreed to read all of these essays, doing so with great care. During the preparation of this book, my department chair, Gaines M. Foster, always responded positively to my requests. With unflagging enthusiasm, Jacqueline Blair, a former LSU undergraduate, prepared the manuscript for publication. Rand Dotson, American history editor at LSU Press, enthusiastically embraced my proposal for this book. With good cheer, Patricia Holmes Cooper has permitted Jefferson Davis to occupy what has seemingly become a permanent space in our home. But, of course, the book is mine, and I accept full responsibility for it.

NOTES

ABBREVIATIONS USED IN NOTES

JD   Jefferson Davis

JDA   William J. Cooper Jr., *Jefferson Davis, American* (New York, 2000).

JDC   Dunbar Rowland, ed., *Jefferson Davis, Constitutionalist: His Letters, Papers and Speeches,* 10 vols. (Jackson, Miss., 1923).

JDE   William J. Cooper Jr., ed., *Jefferson Davis: The Essential Writings* (New York 2003).

LC   Division of Manuscripts, Library of Congress, Washington, D.C.

MC   Eleanor S. Brockenbrough Library, Museum of the Confederacy, Richmond, Va.

Memoir   Varina Howell Davis, *Jefferson Davis, Ex-President of the Confederate States of America: A Memoir by His Wife,* 2 vols. (New York, 1890).

M&P   James D. Richardson, comp., *A Compilation of the Messages and Papers of the Confederacy . . . ,* 2 vols. (Nashville, 1906).

OR   *War of the Rebellion: A Compilation of the Official Records of the Union and Confederate Armies,* 70 vols. in 128 parts (Washington, D.C., 1880–1901).

PJD   Lynda L. Crist et al., eds., *The Papers of Jefferson Davis,* 12 vols. (Baton Rouge, 1971–).

UNC   Southern Historical Collection, Wilson Library, University of North Carolina, Chapel Hill, N.C.

1. *JDA.*

2. For a full citation to the previously published essay, see chap. 1, note 1.

1. JEFFERSON DAVIS AND THE SUDDEN DISAPPEARANCE
OF SOUTHERN POLITICS

1. Edward A. Pollard, *Life of Jefferson Davis, With a Secret History of the Southern Confederacy, Gathered "Behind the Scenes in Richmond"* (Philadelphia, 1869); *Memoir,* 2:12. This essay first appeared in Charles Eagles, ed., *Is There a Southern Political Tradition?* (Jackson, Miss., 1996), 27–42. It appears here with minor alterations; also the notes have been reformatted for this volume.

2. Bell I. Wiley, *The Road to Appomattox* (1956; reprint, Baton Rouge, 1994), chap. 1 (quotes, 17, 29); Allan Nevins, *Ordeal of the Union,* 2 vols. (New York, 1947); Nevins, *Emergence of Lincoln,* 2 vols. (New York, 1950); Nevins, *War for the Union,* 4 vols. (New York, 1959–71); David M. Potter, "Jefferson Davis and the Political Factors in Confederate Defeat," in David Donald, ed., *Why the North Won the Civil War* (Baton Rouge, 1960), 91–112.

3. Paul D. Escott, *Jefferson Davis and the Failure of Confederate Nationalism* (Baton Rouge, 1978); George C. Rable, *The Confederate Republic: A Revolution against Politics* (Chapel Hill, 1994); William C. Davis, *Jefferson Davis: The Man and His Hour* (New York, 1991), 447 (quote).

4. Ludwell Johnson, "Jefferson Davis and Abraham Lincoln as War Presidents: Nothing Succeeds Like Success," *Civil War History* 27 (Mar. 1981): 49–63. For examples of scholars who recognize Davis's problems in addition to pointing out his shortcomings, see J. G. Randall and David Donald, *The Civil War and Reconstruction,* 2d rev. ed. (Lexington, Mass., 1969), 272–73; and James McPherson, *Ordeal by Fire: The Civil War and Reconstruction,* 2d ed. (New York, 1992), 362–63.

5. Roy Nichols, *Franklin Pierce: Young Hickory of the Granite Hills,* 2d ed. (Philadelphia, 1958), 537.

6. "Extracts from an Autobiographical Sketch," *PJD,* 2:697.

7. Andrew Johnson to George W. Jones, Mar. 13, 1860, in Paul H. Bergeron et al., eds., *The Papers of Andrew Johnson,* 16 vols. (Knoxville, 1967–2000), 3:467; Reuben Davis, *Recollections of Mississippi and Mississippians* (Boston and New York, 1891), 193; Varina Davis to [Margaret K. Howell], Sept. 5, 1845, JD Papers, W. S. Hoole Special Collections Library, University of Alabama, Tuscaloosa.

8. Varina Davis to Margaret K. Howell, June 6, 1846, *PJD,* 2:641–42; JD to Varina Davis, May 8, 1851, ibid., 4:181.

9. JD to Stephen Cocke, Nov. 30, 1847, ibid., 3:248; Albert G. Brown to J. F. H. Claiborne, June 7, 1855, J. F. H. Claiborne Papers, UNC.

10. [Collin S. Tarpley], *A Sketch of Jeff. Davis, the Democratic Candidate for Governor* (Jackson, Miss., 1851); *Harper's Weekly*, Jan. 9, 1858; *Speeches of the Hon. Jefferson Davis of Mississippi, Delivered during the Summer of 1858 . . .* (Baltimore, 1859); Mississippi citizens to JD, Oct. 1, 1858, and Collin S. Tarpley to JD, Dec. 1, 1858, *PJD*, 6:586–87; JD to J. L. M. Curry, June 4, 1859, ibid., 253; Varina Davis to JD, Apr. 17, 1859, ibid., 244.

11. *PJD*, 2:xxxiv–xxxvii; ibid., 4:xxxvi–xxxvii; Varina Davis to William E. Dodd, Mar. 10, 1905, William E. Dodd Papers, LC; Davis, *Recollections*, 193.

12. *PJD*, 6:xlviii, liv–lv. A prime example is the illness that drastically curtailed Davis's gubernatorial campaign in 1851.

13. JD to Eli Abbott, Dec. 21, 1845, ibid., 2:399; JD to George Bancroft, Dec. 12, 1845, ibid., 381; Smith to JD, Feb. 2, 1849, ibid., 4:10. See also *Vicksburg Whig*, Jan. 6, 1846.

14. JD to Stephen Cocke, Nov. 30, 1847, *PJD*, 3:249. The ledger is in the JD Papers, Special Collections, Howard-Tilton Memorial Library, Tulane University, New Orleans.

15. *Vicksburg Sentinel*, Nov. 15, 1843, July 11, 1845; JD to Franklin Pierce, June 13, 1860, *JDC*, 4:495–96; L. Q. C. Lamar to C. H. Mott, May 29, 1860, in Edward Mayes, *Lucius Q. C. Lamar: His Life, Times, and Speeches, 1823–1893*, 2d ed. (Nashville, 1896), 83.

16. JD to E. C. Wilkinson, Sept. 17, 1851, *JDC*, 2:86; ibid., 3:132, 4:62; *PJD*, 4:268.

17. JD to Stephen Cocke, Dec. 19, 1853, *JDC*, 2:335.

18. JD to [Ethelbert] Barksdale and [Franklin C.] Jones, Feb. 2, 1848, *PJD*, 4:248.

19. On Davis, the Democrats, and Taylor, see JD to Robert J. Walker, June 29, 1847, and JD to [Simon Cameron], July 26, 1847, *PJD*, 3:190–91, 196–97; and Frank Blair to Martin Van Buren, Feb. 29, 1848, Martin Van Buren Papers, LC. For public addresses, consult the *Jackson Mississippian*, Sept. 29, 1848; and *PJD*, 3:375. Davis's private views can be found in JD to Beverly Tucker, Apr. 12, 1848, *PJD*, 3:292.

20. "Autobiographical Sketch," *PJD*, 2:700. See also ibid., 694 n5, 3:3.

21. For Davis's unsuccessful struggle, see the *Congressional Globe* for the first session of the Thirty-first Congress; *PJD*, vol. 4; and especially *JDC*, vol. 1 (which reprints many of his speeches). One in which he acknowledges the outcome is in *JDC*, 1:482.

22. For example, see JD to Lowndes County Citizens, Nov. 22, 1850, *PJD*, 4:138–45. On Mississippi and the compromise generally, the most thorough study remains Cleo Hearon, "Mississippi and the Compromise of 1850," *Publications of the Mississippi Historical Society* 14 (1914): 7–229.

23. The public statement is in *PJD*, 4:231; and the private opinion is in JD to ? [Aug.–Oct. 1852], ibid., 293–97 (quote, 297).

24. *JDC*, 1:378, 509, 3:358; *PJD*, 6:154.

25. *JDC*, 3:343.

26. JD to Robert Barnwell Rhett Jr., Nov. 10, 1860, *PJD*, 6:368–70; William T. Walthall Diary, Mar. 3, 1877, William T. Walthall Papers, Mississippi Department of Archives and History, Jackson; Davis [a congressman attending the meeting], *Recollections*, 390–91;

Otho R. Singleton [also a congressman at the meeting] to Davis, July 14, 1877, in JD, *The Rise and Fall of the Confederate Government,* 2 vols. (New York, 1881), 1:58–59.

27. On Davis and Seward, consult *Memoir,* 1:579–83; and Henry Bellows, "Memorandum on Dinner in 1863," Henry Bellows Papers, Massachusetts Historical Society, Boston. (I am grateful to Charles Royster for the Bellows reference.)

28. "Autobiography," *PJD,* 1:lxi; *New York Herald,* Dec. 23, 27, 1860; Samuel S. Cox, *Eight Years in Congress, 1857–1865: Memoir and Speeches* (New York, 1865), 27.

29. Davis to Anna Ella Carroll, Mar. 1, 1861, *PJD,* 7:65; JD to Pierce, Jan. 20, 1861, *JDC,* 5:37–38; *PJD,* 7:18–22; *New York Herald,* Jan. 22, 1861; Myrta Lockett Avary, *Dixie after the War: An Exposition of Social Conditions Existing in the South, during the Twelve Years Succeeding the Fall of Richmond* (New York, 1906), 414–15.

30. Elizabeth Blair Lee to Philip, Jan. 21, 1861, in Virginia Jeans Laas, ed., *Wartime Washington: The Civil War Letters of Elizabeth Blair Lee* (Urbana and Chicago, 1991), 27; Caroline Philips Myers Manuscript Memoir, Phillips-Myers Papers, UNC; Gwin to J. F. H. Claiborne, Nov. 14, 1878, Claiborne Papers, UNC.

31. *JDC,* 5:49–53, 67–85 (quote, 53).

32. Rable, *Confederate Republic;* Eric H. Walther, *The Fire-Eaters* (Baton Rouge, 1992).

33. JD to Stephen Cocke, Nov. 30, 1847, *PJD,* 3:248–49; ibid., 6:198; Eli N. Evans, *Judah P. Benjamin: The Jewish Confederate* (New York, 1988), 99.

2. JEFFERSON DAVIS AND THE POLITICS OF SECESSION

1. For example, see Kenneth M. Stampp, *America in 1857: A Nation on the Brink* (New York, 1990), 4; and Michael A Morrison, *Slavery and the American West: The Eclipse of Manifest Destiny and the Coming of the Civil War* (Chapel Hill, 1997), 211–12. For details on Davis's activity during the period covered in this essay, see *JDA,* chaps. 7–10.

2. *JDC,* 3:358.

3. Polk to Robert Armstrong, June 13, 1847, James K. Polk Papers, LC.

4. The best book on the years between the Mexican War and the Civil War remains David M. Potter's superb, *The Impending Crisis, 1848–1861,* comp. and ed. Don E. Fehrenbacher (New York, 1976), which provides ample background and general coverage for the matters discussed in this essay. I will not cite it constantly.

5. *PJD,* 3:332, 334.

6. Ibid., 347–48; *JDC,* 1:509.

7. Clyde N. Wilson et al., eds. *The Papers of John C. Calhoun,* 28 vols. (Columbia, S.C., 1959–2003), 26:235.

8. *PJD,* 3:367.

9. *JDC,* 1:486.

10. Ibid., 2:42; *PJD,* 4:141.

11. The speeches: *JDC,* 3:271–73 (on shipboard; quote, 273), 274–81, 284–88, 288–95, 305–15, *PJD,* 6:214–23.

12. *PJD,* 6:207n3; James Byrne Ranck, *Albert Gallatin Brown: Radical Southern Nationalist* (New York, 1937), 163; *Vicksburg Daily Whig,* Sept. 14, Oct. 12, 1858.

13. *Speeches of the Hon. Jefferson Davis of Mississippi, Delivered during the Summer of 1858 . . .* (Baltimore, 1859).

14. JD to J. L. M. Curry, June 4, 1859, *PJD,* 6:253–54. For JD's resolutions, see ibid, 273–75; and *JDC,* 4:203–4. Even David Potter has Davis wanting a slave code. *Impending Crisis, 1848–1861,* comp. and ed. Don E. Fehrenbacher (New York, 1976), 403–04. I want to note, however, that William W. Freehling is on point with JD's resolutions and his differences with Brown. *The Road to Disunion: Secessionists Triumphant, 1854–1861* (New York, 2007), 275–76.

15. *PJD,* 6:228 (first and second quotes); *Vicksburg Weekly Whig,* Nov. 14, 1860 (third quote).

16. *JDC,* 4:158; *PJD,* 6:364–66.

17. JD to Robert Barnwell Rhett Jr., Nov. 10, 1860, *PJD,* 6:368–70; *JDA,* 340.

18. I am convinced that Davis's major hope for a deal between Republicans and the South rested on his relationship with William H. Seward, the influential Republican senator from New York. In the late 1850s the two men had established a friendship based on a mutual respect. Furthermore, according to Davis's wife, Seward had told both her husband and her that much of what he said was for political effect. But no as yet discovered contemporary evidence reveals any private discussion or correspondence between the two men in November–December 1860. *Memoir,* 1:547–83. See also Henry Bellows, "Memorandum on Dinner in 1863," Henry Bellows Papers, Massachusetts Historical Society, Boston. (I am grateful to Charles Royster for the Bellows reference.)

19. JD to Frank H. Alfriend, Aug. 17, 1867, *JDE,* 394; Caroline P. Myers Manuscript Memoir, Phillips-Myers Papers, UNC.

3. JEFFERSON DAVIS AND STATES' RIGHTS IN THE CONFEDERACY

1. Frank L. Owsley, *State Rights in the Confederacy* (Chicago, 1925). For a recent historiographical treatment, see George C. Rable's illuminating, "Beyond State Rights: The Shadowy World of Confederate Politics," in James M. McPherson and William J. Cooper Jr., eds., *Writing the Civil War: The Quest to Understand* (Columbia, S.C., 1998), 135–53.

2. Charles M. Wiltse, *John C. Calhoun,* 3 vols. (Indianapolis, 1944–51), 3:234–45.

3. *PJD,* 2:501

4. *JDC,* 3:358; *JDE,* 190.

5. *PJD,* 5:30–31.

6. *JDC,* 3:363–76.

7. *M&P,* 1:37, 63; *JDE,* 199.

8. *JDC,* 6:61, 338–40.

9. *M&P,* 1:205–6. *Correspondence between Governor Brown and President Davis on the Constitutionality of the Conscription Act* (Atlanta, 1862) contains the lengthy missives between the two men.

10. George C. Rable, *The Confederate Republic: A Revolt against Politics* (Chapel Hill, 1994).

11. *M&P,* 1:348; *JDC,* 6:357, 358.

12. On JD and Vance, consult *JDA,* 477–78.

13. Henry S. Foote, *Casket of Reminiscences* (1874; reprint: New York, 1968), 292; Shelby Foote, *The Civil War: A Narrative,* 3 vols. (New York, 1958–74), 2:950; Robert Toombs to Alexander Stephens, July 19, 1863, Alexander H. Stephens Papers, Special Collections Department, Robert W. Woodruff Library, Emory University, Atlanta; Myrton Lockett Avary, *Recollections of Alexander H. Stephens . . .* (New York, 1910), 168–69; L. Stephens to A. H. Stephens, Apr. 6, 1863, Alexander H. Stephens Papers, Manhattanville College, Purchase, N.Y.

4. JEFFERSON DAVIS AND THE POLITICS OF CONFEDERATE COMMAND

1. *JDC,* 1:303.

2. Caroline P. Myers Manuscript Memoir, Phillips-Myers Papers, UNC.

3. *M&P,* 1:82.

4. JD to William P. Johnston, Nov. 18, 1877, and JD to Jubal Early, Apr. 7, 1878, *JDE,* 420, 422.

5. For an excellent review of the literature, consult Emory M. Thomas, "Rebellion and Conventional Warfare: Confederate Strategy and Military Policy," in James M. McPherson and William J. Cooper Jr., eds., *Writing the Civil War: The Quest to Understand* (Columbia, S.C., 1998), 36–59.

6. JD to Edmund Kirby Smith, Nov. 19, 1863, and JD to William P. Johnston, Nov. 18, 1877, *JDE,* 329, 420.

7. Edmund Kirby Smith to JD, June 16, Sept. 5, 1863, *PJD,* 9:222, 372; JD to H. Flanigan, July 15, 1863, *JDC,* 5:565–66.

8. JD to Jubal Early, Apr. 7, 1878, *JDE,* 422.

9. Isham Harris to JD, July 13, 1861, and JD to Harris, July 17, 1861, *PJD,* 7:241, 246.

10. JD to Francis W. Pickens, Aug. 1, 1862, ibid., 8:318.

11. JD to Edmund Kirby Smith, July 14, 1863, *JDE,* 307.

12. JD to Isham Harris, July 17, 1861, *PJD,* 7:246; *JDE,* 281.

13. *PJD,* 9:8.

14. Johnston to JD, Sept. 12, 1861, *OR,* ser. 4, 1:605–8 (calendared, *PJD,* 7:336); Craig L. Symonds, *Joseph E. Johnston: A Civil War Biography* (New York, 1992), 128.

15. JD to Johnston, Sept. 14, 1861, *PJD,* 7:340.

16. *OR,* ser. 1, 2:484–504.

17. JD to Beauregard, Oct. 20, 30, 1861, *JDC,* 5:148, 156–57.

18. Beauregard to Gen. Samuel Cooper, May 19, 1862, *OR,* ser. 1, 10(2):530.

19. JD to Varina Davis, June 19, 1862, *PJD,* 8:254; Stephen R. Mallory Diary, June 21, 1862, Stephen R. Mallory Papers, UNC.

20. Beauregard to Thomas Jordan, July 12, 1862, Letterbook, P. G. T. Beauregard Papers, LC.

21. JD to Joseph Davis, June 18, 1861, *PJD,* 7:204.

22. JD to William J. Hardee, Oct. 30, 1863, *JDC,* 6:72.

5. JEFFERSON DAVIS AND THE POLITICAL DIMENSIONS OF CONFEDERATE STRATEGY

1. See, for example, the enormously influential David M. Potter, "Jefferson Davis and the Political Factors in Confederate Defeat," in David Donald, ed., *Why the North Won the Civil War* (Baton Rouge, 1960), 91–112. Mark E. Neely Jr. has a helpful review of the literature in his "Abraham Lincoln and Jefferson Davis: Comparing Presidential Leadership in the Civil War," in James M. McPherson and William J. Cooper Jr., eds., *Writing the Civil War: The Quest to Understand* (Columbia, S.C., 1998), 96–111.

2. *Harper's Weekly,* Jan. 9, 1858.

3. For JD's antebellum political career, consult *JDA,* chaps. 6–10; *Memoir,* 2:12; JD to Alexander M. Clayton, Jan. 30, 1861, *PJD,* 7:27–28. See also chap. 1 herein.

4. On the presidential selection, William C. Davis finds more competition than I can discern. See his *"A Government of Our Own": The Making of the Confederacy* (New York, 1994), chap. 5.

5. Potter, "Davis and the Political Factors."

6. For the events leading up to Fort Sumter, see David M. Potter, *The Impending Conflict, 1848–1861,* comp. and ed. Don E. Fehrenbacher (New York, 1976), chaps. 19–20.

7. JD to John A. Campbell, Apr. 6, 1861, *PJD,* 7:92–93; *New York Citizen,* May 4, 1867.

8. *JDA,* 364–65; Ulrich B. Phillips, *The Life of Robert Toombs* (New York, 1913), 234–35; JD to Braxton Bragg, Apr. 3, 1861, *PJD,* 7:85.

9. JD to Edmund Kirby Smith, Nov. 19, 1863, *JDE,* 329.

10. For more on JD's desire to carry the war to his enemy and in his understanding of Confederate nationalism, see chaps. 6 and 7.

11. I discuss these matters in more detail in chap. 6.

12. JD to Holmes, Dec. 21, 1862, *JDE,* 274–76; JD to Smith, July 2, 1863, *JDC,* 5:534.

13. JD to Smith, Nov. 19, 1863, *JDE,* 329.

14. JD to Lee, May 31, 1863, *PJD,* 9:202.

15. Emory M. Thomas, *Robert E. Lee: A Biography* (New York, 1995), 288–89; Thomas Lawrence Connelly and Archer Jones, *The Politics of Command: Factions and Ideas in*

Confederate Strategy (Baton Rouge, 1973), 49–66; *JDA,* 436–37; John H. Reagan, *Memoirs, with Special Reference to Secession and the Civil War* (Washington and New York, 1908), 120–23.

16. Lee to James A. Seddon, May 10, 1863, in Clifford Dowdey and Louis H. Manarin, eds., *The Wartime Papers of R. E. Lee* (Boston and Toronto, 1961), 482.

17. JD to Dabney Maury, Dec. 17, 1877, JD Papers, MC.

6. JEFFERSON DAVIS AND THE WAR IN THE WEST

1. For a thoughtful discussion of the literature, see Emory M. Thomas, "Rebellion and Conventional Warfare: Confederate Strategy and Military Policy," in James M. McPherson and William J. Cooper Jr., eds., *Writing the Civil War: The Quest to Understand* (Columbia, S.C., 1998), 36–59.

2. *JDC,* 8:232 (first quote); W. P. Johnston to Rosa, Aug. 24, 1862 (second quote), Mrs. Mason Barret Collection of the Papers of Albert Sidney and William Preston Johnston, Special Collections, Howard-Tilton Memorial Library, Tulane University, New Orleans.

3. JD, *Rise and Fall of the Confederate Government,* 2 vols. (New York, 1881), 2:67.

4. JD to Bragg, Aug. 5, 1862, *PJD,* 8:322. For detail on the Kentucky campaign, see Thomas Lawrence Connelly, *Army of the Heartland: The Army of Tennessee, 1861–1862* (Baton Rouge, 1967), pt. 5; and Kenneth W. Noe, *Perryville: This Grand Havoc of Battle* (Lexington, Ky., 2001).

5. Craig L. Symonds, *Joseph E. Johnston: A Civil War Biography* (New York, 1992), chap. 14. See also Stephen E. Woodworth, *Jefferson Davis and His Generals: The Failure of Confederate Command in the West* (Lawrence, Kans., 1990), chap. 11; and Thomas Lawrence Connelly, *Autumn of Glory: The Army of Tennessee, 1862–1865* (Baton Rouge, 1971), chap. 5.

6. *Correspondence between the President and General Joseph E. Johnston . . . , during the Months of May, June, and July 1863* (Richmond, 1864), has all pertinent documents (JD to Johnston, May 28, 1863, 10). For more detail and context, consult Woodworth, *Davis and His Generals,* chap. 12; and Michael B. Ballard, *Vicksburg: The Campaign that Opened the West* (Chapel Hill, 2004).

7. Johnston to Lydia Johnston, June 25, 1863 (first quote), John W. Johnston Papers, Rare Books, Manuscript and Special Collections Library, Duke University, Durham, N.C.; Johnston to Lydia Johnston, June 29, 1863 (second quote), McLane-Fisher Papers, Maryland Historical Society, Baltimore (I am grateful to Charles Royster for this reference).

8. JD to Robert Howry, Aug. 27, 1863, *PJD,* 9:357–58.

9. Polk to JD, Oct. 6, 1863, ibid., 10:13. For more detail and context, see Connelly, *Autumn of Glory,* chaps. 9–10; and Woodworth, *Davis and His Generals,* chap. 13.

10. JD to William J. Hardee, Oct. 30, 1863, and JD to Bragg, Oct. 29, 1863, *JDC,* 6:71, 72.

1. Incredibly influential has been David M. Potter, "Jefferson Davis and the Political Factors in Confederate Defeat," in David Donald, ed., *Why the North Won the Civil War* (Baton Rouge, 1960), 91–112. See also Paul D. Escott, *Jefferson Davis and the Failure of Confederate Nationalism* (Baton Rouge, 1978); George C. Rable, *The Confederate Republic: A Revolution against Politics* (Chapel Hill, 1994); and William C. Davis, *Jefferson Davis: The Man and His Hour* (New York, 1991); cf. Ludwell Johnson, "Jefferson Davis and Abraham Lincoln as War Presidents: Nothing Succeeds Like Success," *Civil War History* 27 (1981), 49–63. For general comments, see Mark E. Neely Jr., "Abraham Lincoln vs. Jefferson Davis: Comparing Presidential Leadership in the Civil War," in James M. McPherson and William J. Cooper Jr., eds., *Writing the Civil War: The Quest to Understand* (Columbia, S.C., 1998), 96–111.

2. A recent suggestive treatment of the role of war leader is Eliot A. Cohen, *Supreme Command: Soldiers, Statesmen, and Leadership in Wartime* (New York, 2002), which argues for a leader intimately involved with his generals.

3. C. Vann Woodward, ed. *Mary Chesnut's Civil War* (New Haven, 1981), 83 (quote); William C. Davis, *"A Government of Our Own:" The Making of the Confederacy* (New York: 1994), 212–13.

4. JD to William M. Brooks, Mar. 15, 1862 (first quote), and JD to John Forsyth, July 18, 1862 (second quote), *PJD,* 8:100, 294.

5. JD to Jubal Early, Apr. 7, 1878, *JDE,* 422.

6. JD to W. P. Johnston, Nov. 18, 1877, and JD to Edmund Kirby Smith, Nov. 19, 1863, ibid., 329 (second quote), 420 (first quote).

7. Ibid., 288. Gary Gallagher emphasizes the critical role of the army. *The Confederate War: How Popular Will, Nationalism, and Military Strategy Could Not Stave off Defeat* (Cambridge, Mass., 1997), chap. 2. See also Drew Gilpin Faust's insightful *The Creation of Confederate Nationalism: Ideology and Identity in the Civil War South* (Baton Rouge, 1988).

8. *JDE,* 199.

9. *M&P,* 1:277.

10. *JDC,* 6:359.

11. John H. Reagan, *Memoirs, with Special Reference to Secession and the Civil War* (Washington and New York, 1906), 164; *JDC,* 6:61.

12. Robert E. Lee (at this time military adviser to the president and writing for the president) to Joseph Johnston, June 7, 1861, *OR,* ser. 1, 2:910; JD to Polk, Sept. 6, 1861, *PJD,* 7:327.

13. JD to A. S. Johnston, Mar. 12, 26, 1862, *PJD,* 7:92–94, 117; JD to Theophilus Holmes, Dec. 21, 1862, Jan. 28, 1863, *JDE,* 274–76, 292–94.

14. JD to Braxton Bragg, Aug. 5, 1862, *JDE,* 259.

15. See *JDA,* esp. chaps. 11–15.

1. The best guide to this critical period remains David M. Potter, *The Impending Crisis, 1848–1861*, comp. and ed. by Don E. Fehrenbacher (New York, 1976).

2. *PJD*, 3:315; *JDC*, 1:316; JD to Dr. Samuel A. Cartwright, June 10, 1849, *PJD*, 4:22–23.

3. *PJD*, 3:347–48.

4. Ibid., 332–34; Charles M. Wiltse, *John C. Calhoun*, 3 vols. (Indianapolis, 1944–51), 2:269–70.

5. *JDE*, 190.

6. *JDC*, 4:85–86.

7. *JDE*, 190–94 (quote, 193).

8. Ibid., 198–203 (quote, 199).

9. Ibid., 197. On the intimate connection between liberty and slavery, see William J. Cooper Jr., *Liberty and Slavery: Southern Politics to 1860* (New York, 1983).

10. *M&P*, 1:268, 290.

11. Ibid., 290–91.

12. *JDE*, 199. On JD's attackers, see chap. 3.

13. See chap. 3.

14. JD to William Smith, Mar. 30, 1865, *JDE*, 361; *JDA*, 556–58.

15. JD, *Rise and Fall of the Confederate Government*, 2 vols. (New York, 1881).

16. JD to [J. P.] Knott, Jan. 22, 1876 (typescript), Correspondence by Author, Tennessee State Library and Archives, Nashville; JD to James Lyons, May 15, 1879, James Lyons Papers, UNC.

17. See chap. 9.

18. JD, *Rise and Fall*, 1:80.

1. For the election, notification, and journey to Montgomery, see *JDA*, 326–29; and *New York Herald*, Feb. 18, 1861 (quote).

2. For JD in Montgomery, see *JDA*, 353–56; *JDC*, 5:48–49 (which contains the evening remarks); *JDE*, 198–203 (for the inaugural); and JD to Varina Davis, Feb. 20, 1861, *PJD*, 7:54. On the intimacy between black slavery and white liberty, see William J. Cooper Jr., *Liberty and Slavery: Southern Politics to 1860* (New York, 1983).

3. For biographical detail, see *JDA*, chaps. 16–19.

4. *Richmond Dispatch*, Mar. 27, 1886; R. G. Spalding to JD, Mar. 19, 1886, JD Papers, MC; *JDC*, 9:419–23 (quote, 419).

5. *JDC*, 9:419–23 (quote, 421).

6. Ibid., 426–27 (quote, 427); Clay-Clopton to "My dear Anne," Nov. 3, 1904 (typescript), Walter Lynwood Fleming Papers, New York Public Library.

7. *JDC*, 9:129–30 (quotes, 429).

8. Ibid., 432–38 (quotes, 433, 434, 435, 436, 437).

9. Ibid., 420 (first quote); Howell Cobb to William Henry Seward, July 18, 1865 (third quote), Cobb to Daniel Sickles, Sept. 12, 1866 (second quote), Ulrich Bonnell Phillips, ed., *The Correspondence of Robert Toombs, Alexander H. Stephens, and Howell Cobb* (Washington, D.C., 1913), 663–65, 682–84.

10. For insightful treatments of the Lost Cause ideology in its political and cultural context, consult Gaines M. Foster, *Ghosts of the Confederacy: Defeat, the Lost Cause, and the Emergence of the New South* (New York, 1987); and David W. Blight, *Race and Reunion: The Civil War in American Memory* (Cambridge, Mass., 2001). For specific mention of Davis pertaining to this essay, see Foster, 95–96, and Blight, 259–60. For more detail on Davis, consult Donald E. Collins, *The Death and Resurrection of Jefferson Davis* (Lanham, Md., 2005), chap. 2.

11. *JDE*, 190–94 (the farewell); *M&P*, 1:66–68 (the message; quote, 68). Two studies that leave no doubt that southern concerns about slavery were of crucial importance for secession are Charles Dew, *The Apostles of Slavery: Southern Secession Commissioners and the Causes the Civil War* (Charlottesville, 2000), 78 (Georgian quote); and William W. Freehling, *The Road to Disunion: Secessionists Triumphant, 1854–1861* (New York, 2007).

INDEX

Calhoun, John C. *(continued)*
72–77; deserters during, 84–85; failed
Confederate advance into Kentucky
during, 70–77, 87, 88; and Lee's plans for
offensive into the North, 64–66; material limitations of Confederacy in, 81;
meaning of, and Davis, 91–100; military
appointments by Davis during, 45–47,
53–54, 61, 68–69; plantations of Davis
brothers overrun by Union soldiers
during, 16; and political dimensions
of Confederate strategy, 55–66; and
politics of Confederate military command, 41–54, 69–70; prisoners of war
in, 96; and slave soldiers in Confederate Army, 81, 84, 97–98; strategic fundamentals of Confederate command during, 44–45, 53–54, 60–66, 82; and theater
commands, 62, 69; Trans-Mississippi
theater of, 44, 45, 47, 61–63, 74; in the
West, 50, 61–62, 67–77. *See also* Civil
War battles
Civil War battles: Chancellorsville,
64; Chickamauga, 70, 75, 76; First
Manassas, 51; Fort Sumter, 15, 36–37,
43, 47, 51, 58–59, 61; Missionary Ridge,
53; Murfreesboro, 72; Perryville, 71;
Shiloh, 53, 69; Vicksburg defense,
61–64, 73–75. *See also* Civil War
Clay, Henry, 32
Clay-Clopton, Virginia, 105
Committee of Thirteen, 13–14, 31–32
Compromise of 1850, 8, 11–12, 23–25, 91
Concentration, as military principle,
44–45, 82
Confederate Army: and Army of Northern Virginia, 64; and Army of Tennessee, 37, 50, 51, 53, 70–73, 75–77, 88; command relationships between Davis and
generals in, 48–54, 70–77, 80, 86–89; and
concentration principle, 44–45, 82; and

conscription, 37–39, 81, 84, 97; Davis as
commander in chief of, 70–77, 79–89;
and Department of East Tennessee,
70; and Department of Mississippi and
Southeast Louisiana, 61–62, 73–74; and
Department of the West, 50, 61–62,
68–69, 72–77; desertions by soldiers
in, 84–85; enlistments in, 37, 80; and
failed advance into Kentucky, 70–77,
87, 88; Lee's plans for offensive into
the North, 64–66; major military appointments by Davis to, 45–47, 53–54,
61, 68–69; material limitations of, 81;
slave soldiers in, 81, 84, 97–98; and strategic fundamentals of Confederate
command, 44–45, 53–54, 60–66, 82; and
theater commands, 62, 69; and Trans-
Mississippi theater, 44, 45, 47, 61–63, 74;
and Vicksburg defense, 61–64, 73–75;
and western theater, 67–77. *See also*
Civil War; Civil War battles; and specific generals
Confederate Congress: and conscription, 38, 81, 84; and Davis on Republican Party, 108; and Davis on sovereign
states of Confederacy, 36; and Davis's
commitment to Confederacy, 43; and
Emancipation Proclamation, 96; and
enlistments in Confederate Army, 37,
81; and military appointments, 48–49;
support for Davis by, 40, 97
Confederate soldiers monument (Montgomery, Ala.), 101–2, 104–8
Confederate States of America: cabinet of, 16, 59, 65; command relationships between Davis and generals in,
48–54, 70–77, 80, 86–89; compared with
American Revolution, 14–15, 82–83, 95,
103–4; Constitution of, 36–38, 40, 43, 79,
97; creation of, 14, 36, 42, 57, 61, 80, 95;
Davis as commander in chief in, 70–77,

79–89; Davis selected as president of, 14, 56, 95, 102; Davis's devotion to, 15–17, 38–39, 42–43, 48, 54; Davis's leadership style in, 15–17, 86–89; and Davis's trips to western theater, 69–70, 72, 73–74, 76, 85; goal of, as independence and liberty, 14–15, 82–84, 95, 97, 100; inauguration of Davis as president of, 36, *following p. 54*, 95, 97, 101–4, 107; military appointments by Davis, 45–47, 53–54, 61, 68–69; military linked with politics in, 43–54, 56–66, 69–70; nationalism of, 45, 60–61, 81–82; politics of, and Davis's authority as president, 15–17, 38–40, 42–54, 56–66, 89; and prisoners of war, 96; relief efforts by, 84; and states' rights, 36–40, 97, 106; tax policy of, 84. *See also* Civil War; Confederate Congress; Davis, Jefferson; Lost Cause ideology; Secession

Congress, Confederate. *See* Confederate Congress

Congress, U.S.: and California statehood, 23–24; Committee of Thirteen in, 13–14, 31–32; and Compromise of 1850, 8, 11–12, 23–25, 91; and Crittenden Compromise, 13, 32; Davis in, 5, 6–14, 20–25, 26, 31–32, 34–36, 41, 42, 55, 79, 91–95; Davis's farewell speech to Senate of, 14, 32, 34–35, 42, 94–95, 108; equality of South in Senate, 20, 24; and Kansas-Nebraska Act, 26, 91; and Missouri Compromise, 21, 22, 24, 26, 32, 91; and slavery in territories, 21–25, 26, 29, 91–93; and Walker Tariff, 11; and Wilmot Proviso, 21, 24

Conscription, 37–39, 81, 84, 97

Constitution, Confederate, 36–38, 40, 43, 79, 97

Constitution, U.S.: and national defense, 37–38; on president as commander in chief, 79; and secession, 12, 19, 28, 98–100; and slavery, 42, 92; and states'

rights, 20, 33–34, 40, 93–94, 100; and transcontinental railroad, 36

Cooper, Samuel, 49

Crittenden, John J., 13, 32

Crittenden Compromise, 13, 32

Custom House (Richmond, Va.), *following p. 54*

Davis, Jefferson: as antebellum politician, 5–14, 16–17, 20–32, 55–56, 91–95; books owned by, 42; compared with Lincoln, 4, 45, 50, 57, 61, 70, 80, 87–88; and Confederate soldiers monument in Montgomery, Ala., 101–2, 104–8; death of first wife of, 6; death of son of, 16; Democratic Party loyalty by, 10–11, 33–34, 56; and devotion to Confederacy, 15–17, 42–43, 48, 54; and devotion to Union, 12, 14, 19, 22, 25, 27–28, 42; early military career of, 41, 79; and failed run for Mississippi governor in 1851, 7, 10, 25, 55; and failed run for Mississippi legislature in 1843, 5, 6; health problems of, 6, 8–9, 22, 27, 42, 52, 68, 101, 111*n*12; imprisonment of, after Civil War, 98, 104, 107; and Lost Cause ideology, 91, 98–100, 107–8; in Maine, 27–28; and meaning of Civil War, 91–100; in Mexican War, 5, 6–7, 20, 22, 42, 55, 79, 87, 92; mistaken view of, as unpolitical, 3, 56–57; monument to, in Richmond, Va., *following p. 54*; negative criticisms of, 3–5, 15–16, 28, 38–40, 44, 47–48, 57, 79–80, 81, 85–86, 97; plantation of, in Mississippi, 16, 41, *following p. 54*, 68, 102; postwar years of, 57, 98–100, 104–8; as presidential elector in 1844, 5, 6, 8, 41, 55; refusal of, to ask for pardon, 98–99; residence of, in Richmond, Va., *following p. 54; Rise and Fall of the Confederate Government* by, 57, 98, 99, 104; and

Davis, Jefferson *(continued)*
secession, 12–14, 19–32, 41–42, 48, 94,
98–100; second wife of, 3, 6–7, 8, 14, 56–
57, 104; and slavery, 22–23, 42, 83, 92–95,
96, 99–100, 103–4; and states' rights, 11,
20, 28, 33–40, 93–95, 97, 100, 106; in U.S.
Congress, 5, 6–14, 20–25, 26, 31–32, 34–
36, 41, 42, 55, 79, 91–95; as war secretary
in Pierce administration, 25–26, 35–36,
55, 79, 86, 91, 97. *See also* Civil War;
Confederate States of America
Davis, Joseph, 6, 16, 52, 99
Davis, Varina, 3, 6–7, 8, 14, 56–57, 104
Davis, William C., 4, 115*n*4
Declaration of Independence, 95, 103. *See
also* American Revolution
Democratic Party: and Compromise of
1850, 25; Davis's loyalty to, 10–11, 33–34,
56; divisions within, in Mississippi,
28–29; and popular sovereignty regard-
ing slavery, 23; and presidential election
of 1860, 30–31; and states' rights, 11, 93
Department of East Tennessee, 70
Department of Mississippi and South-
east Louisiana, 61–62, 73–74
Department of the West, 50, 61–62,
68–69, 72–77
Dorsey, Sarah, 104
Douglas, Stephen A., 24, 26, 29–30
Dred Scott decision, 26, 27, 29, 93

Emancipation Proclamation, 83, 96
Escott, Paul, 4

Fire-eaters, 13, 19, 28–29, 31, 94. *See also*
Secession
Florida, 52–53
Foote, Henry S., 39
Fort Monroe, 104
Fort Sumter, 15, 36–37, 43, 47, 51, 58–59, 61
Fourteenth Amendment, 99

Freehling, William W., 113*n*14
Free-soil proposition, 21–22, 26

Generals. *See* specific generals
Georgia, 37, 39, 40, 85–86
Grant, Ulysses S., 62, 74, 75
Gwin, William, 14

Harpers Ferry, 48, 87
Harper's Weekly, 7, 56
Harris, Isham, 46, 48
Holmes, Theophilus, 61–63, 74, 87

Internal improvements, 34

Jackson, Andrew, 34, 42
Jackson, Stonewall, 107
Jackson Mississippian, 28
Jefferson, Thomas, 20, 33, 42, 93
Jefferson Davis Monument (Richmond,
Va.), *following p. 54*
Johnson, Andrew, 6
Johnson, Ludwell, 4
Johnston, Albert Sidney, 49, 51, 53, 68–69,
77, 87
Johnston, Joseph E., 48–51, 53, 54, 61–65,
69, 72–77, 87–88, 107

Kansas-Nebraska Act, 26, 91
Kentucky, 70–77, 87, 88

Lecompton Constitution, 26
Lee, Robert E., 49, 64–66, 67, 69, 99, 107
Lincoln, Abraham: compared with Davis,
4, 45, 50, 57, 61, 70, 80, 87–88; election of,
12, 31, 42, 94; and Emancipation Proclamation, 83, 96; and Fort Sumter, 58;
military appointments by, 45; relationship between generals and, 87–88; on
slavery, 42
Longstreet, James, 76